I0123361

RESTORING
AMERICA

*12 Principles that will Save our
Country, Communities & Families*

Dustin Harris & Joe Olivas
United in Liberty

This work is dedicated to:
Jazmine, CaRynn, Isaac, Joseph, Dallin, Carter, and Eli.

May our generation live by the principles
outlined in this book, that your generation will
not have to fight to restore them.

If you have purchased this book without a cover you should be aware that this work may have been stolen property and reported as "unsold and destroyed" to the publisher. In such case, neither the author nor the publisher has received payment for this "stripped work."

No part of this book may be reproduced or transmitted in any form or means, electronic or mechanical, including photocopying, recording, or by any information storage retrieval systems, without the expressed written consent from the copyright owners. For more information, contact *United in Liberty* Enterprises.

Copyright © 2010 held by *United in Liberty* Enterprises

Published by *United in Liberty* Enterprises, as an imprint of *United in Liberty*.

United in Liberty Enterprises
P.O. Box 1622
Idaho Falls, ID 83403-1622
www.unitedinliberty.org

Printed in the United States of America

Cover design and book layout by BlackBox Graphics
Edited by Tammy Threlfall

FIRST EDITION

ISBN: 978-0-9830856-0-7

SPECIAL SALES
Restoring America is available at special discounts for bulk purchases. For details or more information, contact Special Markets, *United in Liberty* Enterprises, sales@unitedinliberty.org or visit us on the web at www.unitedinliberty.org

AUTHOR'S FOREWORD

It can be a frustrating and even aggravating thing to be involved in your local, state or even national government. It is easy to be angry with the sheer volume of incompetent, dishonest, and just plain unprincipled decisions being made in the halls of lawmaking at every level. As a patriot, you want to feel like you have a voice, but it can be an overwhelming task to say the least. If this describes you, *Restoring America* was written for you.

We, like you, have longed to make a difference and help reshape the course that our country is headed. *Restoring America: 12 Principles that will save our Country, Communities & Families* we believe is the answer. Rather than a top-down approach we advocated a principle-based, bottom-up approach. If you can improve yourself, you can improve your family. When your family has improved, you can help to educate and improve the lives of your neighbors, friends, and co-workers. Once your immediate sphere of influence begins to change, you cannot help but unite in changing your school boards, city councils, community, etc. The city changes the county, the county changes the state and together, the states will change Washington! The silver-tongued politicians at the top levels of congress do not know or perhaps fully understand these principles.

Jefferson advocated for a hands-on political environment. If we will look to the principles taught in 1776 and 1787, we realize that it is not too late to return to our moral and principled base. *Restoring America* is about returning to the truths long ignored.

We hope you enjoy reading *Restoring America* as much as we have enjoyed researching and writing it. If you do, we encourage you to share it with your friends, neighbors, and family. We will only be successful in restoring these principles as we unite with those that feel the same desires and act and become *United in Liberty*!

— Dustin Harris & Joe Olivas

ACKNOWLEDGMENTS

It would be impossible to even begin to thank everyone by name that has contributed in some way to this book. When Adam Smith wrote *An Inquiry into the Nature and Causes of the Wealth of Nations,* he drew heavily upon those great minds of his day and in the past. Later, he was accused of not giving them credit for their ideas. In his defense, Jean Baptiste Say later said, "A man...is indebted to every thing around him; to the scattered lights which he has concentrated, to the errors which he has overthrown, and even to the enemies by whom he has been assailed; inasmuch as they all contribute to the formation of his opinions. But when out of these materials he afterwards forms enlarged views, useful to his contemporaries and posterity, it rather behooves us to acknowledge the extent of our own obligations, than to reproach him with what he has been supplied by others" (*A Treatise on Political Economy*). Though we would never claim to be in the same category as Mr. Smith, the idea is the same. As authors, we have gained wisdom based upon what we read, hear, or watch. This knowledge comes over a period of time and from a plethora of sources. It is not our intention to share any ideas without giving proper credit to their creators, however, this is not always feasible and where possible, sources are given. Most of what is discussed in the pages to follow may have been articulated by others, but are Universal Truths that we inherently know because we are members of the human race.

Of course, it is our Heavenly Father who gave us the knowledge, ability, and everything in which to write this book. He is the Master and we are His instruments. Our wives and children have been our inspiration as well as our support through the formation of United in Liberty and the writing of this book.

A big expression of gratitude must go to Dr. W. Cleon Skousen. It was his research and writings that made this book possible. He (and his dedicated staff), in a time where the Internet was non-existent, painstakingly read, researched, and collected the best from the Founding Fathers. Though the Founders often wrote in ways that were un-derstood by the uneducated farmer in 1776, they are less than casual reading to a modern college graduate. Dr. Skousen took the time and expended the energy to bring this information to light. As you read this book, you will often see quotes that may be familiar from books by Skousen. Often, these quotes were discovered by us in Skousen's books, but whenever possible, the original quotes were researched and stated to their ultimate source. It was Dr. Skousen, however that made this process much easier.

Our thanks to Tammy Threlfall for her painstaking talents and ef-forts in the editing of this important work. Without her truly gifted ability, the many words that have been written might not only be riddled with errors but likewise may have made it difficult for you, the reader, to follow.

And finally, our deepest debt of gratitude goes to the Founding Fathers themselves. You will notice that throughout this book, the Founders are always referred to with capital letters. To us, the phrase "Founding Father" is a title that was earned and paid for with life, for-tunes, and sacred honor. Most of them were called on to lose it all. As much as we would like to hold the Founding Fathers up as infallible demigods, the truth is, in the end, they were just men. They were not perfect. The Lord used them as an instrument to complete His will. It can be argued that after the Constitution was ratified, some of the greatest of the Framers made grave inroads into unconstitutional territory with the Bank of the United States, the Jay Treaty, the Alien and Sedition Acts, the Louisiana Purchase, and others. However, these perceived missteps do not change who they were and what they gave us. Someday, we believe we will meet these men and they will look us in the eyes and ask, "What have you done with the freedom we gave you?" Hopefully, we will not feel like looking at the floor when we give our answer.

CONTENTS

RESTORING AMERICA

12 Principles that will Save our Country, Communities & Families

Dustin Harris & Joe Olivas
United in Liberty

CHAPTER I

How it all begins

"O ye that love mankind! Ye that dare oppose, not only tyranny, but the tyrant, stand forth! 'Tis not in numbers but in unity that our great strength lies." —Thomas Paine

HANGING AS A THREAD

"The general face and state of things, in the interim, will be unsettling and unpromising. Emigrants of property will not choose to come to a country whose form of government hangs but by a thread." —Thomas Paine

When someone is pushed to their very limits, you may hear them utter the phrase, *"I am hanging by a thread."* It does not take much to break a single thread. The same phrase is often used in connection with the freedoms enshrined by the *Constitution*. *"The Constitution is hanging, as it were, by a thread,"* has been the cry recently.

Open any paper, turn on any 24-hour cable channel, or observe in your own neighborhoods and schools, and there is no doubt that we as a nation, have moved far from the principles vouchsafed within the founding documents of our time. The *Constitution*, if you will, is hanging by a thread. It would not take very much at all to break that thread, and once our freedoms are lost, only blood can bring them back. The time is now to rise up as a people and fortify our *Constitution* before it is too late.

A MOVEMENT IS TAKING PLACE

"The laws of God, and of nature, have no dateline…Circumstances do change. So do the problems that are shaped by circumstances. But the principles that govern the solution of the problems do not."
—*Barry Goldwater*

The hand of Providence is moving individuals toward principles of liberty and freedom like never before in history. People are being moved and getting involved where no interest has been felt in the past. Consider the following individual account from one of this book's authors:

"If you had asked me five years ago to read the *Federalist Papers*, I would have scoffed. Though I knew in my heart that I probably should read and study those important documents of history, I truly had no desire. Oh, I was patriotic, sure. I flew my flag, voted in every election, wrote letters to the editor, and even read the *Constitution* and *Declaration of Independence* on an annual basis as one of my personal goals. That, however, was as far as it went.

"That was until a several years ago. Recently, things began to change. Here is the strange thing…the change was not out of my own effort as much as it was from an inward drive. I began to become less and less interested in my spy novels and favorite television shows and more fascinated with history. Specifically, I found myself drawn toward American History. I started to devote all of my free time to books like *The 5,000 Year Leap*, and *The Making of America*. I devoured *The Proper Role of Government* by Benson and Bastiat's *The Law*. *The Real Benjamin Franklin*, *The Real George Washington*, and *The Real Thomas Jefferson* all appealed to me. I could not get enough of the Founding Fathers, their histories, and their writings.

"The more I studied, the more I became disgruntled with what I saw happening around me. For example, I might read a quote by Benson such as, "I hold that the *Constitution* denies government the power to take from the individual either his life, liberty, or property except in accordance with moral law" (*The Proper Role of Government*). As I read, I would awaken to the awful situation I found our nation currently in. I would realize that most everything the government did was about the taking of property (money) from one citizen to re-distribute to another. Not only were we doing the exact opposite of what the proper role of government is, as pointed out by Benson, but we were moving closer and closer to socialism at an alarming rate.

"A funny thing occurs when you begin to become educated. The more you learn, the more disillusioned you get with idleness. No longer could I sit back and allow my country to become corrupt. No longer could I sit by and merely watch as our politicians disregarded and, worse yet, fought openly against these true principles. I had to get involved and I had to do my part.

"The next problem was more complex—what to do exactly? Nothing is more dangerous than a zealot without structure. I began to write my Congressmen. I co-founded a neighborhood newsletter. I united with other, like-minded people to develop a curriculum. I spoke to anyone who would listen, but just felt like a hamster in an exercise wheel. I was busy, but not really doing anything to truly change the situation.

"My awareness of *jogging in place* came to a head one spring day. A group of individuals in my community (and across the country) decided to get together and protest. The ideals and foundations of the protest were sound. The purpose of the rally was to voice our disillusion with a current policy which was blatantly unconstitutional. Because the principles were sound, I felt to be right in the mix of it. I wrote letters to the editor and emailed my friends and family inviting all to join us. I even took a poster board and made a sign (a pretty good one too—if I do say so myself. Okay, my wife helped me). The day for the rally arrived and I showed up at the designated time. Though I had been involved in politics my entire life, I had never participated in a real, honest to goodness protest. This was exciting! This is what *doing something* was all about. The numbers who showed up to the rally were staggering. Far more than I had anticipated came out on a cold, rainy, mid-week evening. We chanted, we listened to speakers, we spoke to the media, we participated, and then we went home…AND THEN WE WENT HOME! That was the problem. We came, we voiced, and we went home. Nothing more was ever done with that group. We did not change a single thing by being there. No policy was changed. No law was passed. No politician was elected. Nothing happened. In a sense, it possibly did more hurt than help. A group of people who believed strongly in a particular topic showed up and, in their mind, *did something*. That night, they went home, patted themselves on the back, and went on with their lives. Do not misunderstand—there is a time and a place for protests. However, if nothing else comes from them other than holding a few signs and, with unity, chanting our displeasure about this thing or that, we have not affected change. We felt like we had done our part, yet no transformation occurred.

"During this time of *stationary biking*, I began to become aware that there were others in the gym. As I spoke with people about true principles of freedom, I found that many around me were having similar feelings. Their lives, and more importantly their hearts, were turning. They were reading the same books I was reading. Conversations about the world around us and Constitutional issues were becoming more and more prevalent. This change was occurring on a wide-scale basis as well. Songs were being written about freedom and were becoming the more popular music on the radio. Web forums and blogs about liberty were popping up at a startling rate. Small and large groups were forming both locally and nationally. In short; good, decent, and patriotic Americans were being moved. I believe that kind of movement occurs only with the help of the hand of the Unseen."

Maybe you have felt similarly. Dante said, "The hottest places in hell are reserved for those who in times of great moral crises maintain their neutrality." You want to do something, but are at a loss as to what to do. It seems that everywhere you turn today, there are new groups cropping up in addition to the many groups who had been around for years. These groups have two things in common. First, they seem to all love freedom and despise the forces working to destroy it. Second, they all have their own, pet agendas. Some are pro-life and others are for legalizing drugs. Some focus on principles of prosperity and others have a fetish for the protection of the Second Amendment. Though each of these groups has a place in honest debate, the problem is that they are disconnected and alone. There needs to be a central group where all patriots can unify under one, freedom-loving banner.

SYNERGY

"Synergy is achieved when two or more people work together to create something better than anyone could alone. It is not your way or my way but a better way, a higher way." —Sean Covey

A wise teacher once taught a memorable lesson about synergy. He took a piece of thread and gave it to a student. He asked that student to break it, and naturally, it was accomplished with ease. The teacher than asked the student (a popular athlete), if he thought he could break that thread again. Confidently, he answered in the affirmative, and the teacher then proceeded to wrap this young man in the thread. With the student's arms to his side, he circled the thread around his body. Around and around he went until the spool was empty. To those in the room, even with the entire spool of thread wrapped around his body, the task did not seem impossible. However, no matter how hard the young man strained, no matter how loud the jeering from his classmates became, he could not break the thread. Conquered, the thread was unwound and the boy returned to his seat in defeat. The moral of the story was this; alone we are weak and prone to fail. Together (like the many wraps of the thread) we are strong and unable to be defeated.

The same problem is being perpetrated on these otherwise successful and patriotic groups. Though most are based on true principles, they are having little, if any affect. Because they hold so tenaciously to their own issues, they are unwilling to combine with, and thus have more affect with other groups. Why would one group who is fighting to keep the family solvent, want to have anything to do with another group who was concerned with border security? Consequently, un-principled changes are occurring in many realms without any real resistance. Laws are being passed, executive orders are being signed, bureaucrats are enforcing rules that no lawmaker ever voted on, and the *Constitution* in general is dissolving at an evermore alarming rate.

The first few times a new whitewater rafter gets out on the river, there can be a learning curve. Often, they will sit in the front of the boat and as the raft approaches a stretch of rapids, they might look at the water, determine the safest route through, and then paddle with all of their strength to obtain the goal. Repeatedly, however, they will find themselves fighting a losing battle. The problem is not the river, or the boat, but rather the lack of unity. The newcomer is not the only one in the boat, but they are paddling as if they were.

Those, even slightly experienced in the art of rafting, know in order to be successful, a rafting group must work together as a team. There is an individual who will sit at the very back of the boat (the anchor-man or guide) who leads the rest of the group. His job is to scan the water ahead, decide the best way to navigate, and then shout orders to the rest of the crew. "Forward paddle, back paddle, right side, paddle, paddle, paddle!" He might bellow. As a crew member, you must learn to put aside your own agenda and trust the guide. That is not easy to do. Often, you may feel that you know better. After all, you are in the front of the boat. Surely you see the river better than he can. How-ever, if you continually paddle when you want to paddle rather than following instructions, you will wear yourself out at best and capsize the boat (putting all in danger) at worse. This would all be completed out of your efforts to do what you thought was best for the whole.

Likewise, there are many different, patriotic groups who are out there striving to navigate the treacherous, political waters. They ac-curately see our freedoms being stripped from us and are doing their best to preserve them. Though they may have the common good of the country in mind, they are failing miserably. They are *paddling* with all of their might, but the boat is capsizing. Why are they failing?

They are failing because they are working alone and are missing the bigger picture. The political raft is not being capsized through one or two rapids (issues). Rather, the boat is sinking due to a combination of many rapids, which together is taking away our freedom.

In this treacherous water, it is wise to remember we are all in the same boat! Ultimately, we are all fighting to uphold and defend the principles enshrined in the *Constitution*. It is even more prudent to remember that we need an anchorman. There must be a guide, a leader who can see the coming stretch of water, fix on a path, and rally the others to work in unison for successfully navigating the raft. Rather than full steam ahead with our own personal group agendas, it is wise to often rally together on this cause or that. By working together to successfully travel the *rapid* of unfair taxation, we may find our own personal *rapid* of religious freedom easier to navigate.

The mission of *United in Liberty*, is not any one particular issue. Rather, our goal is the overall preservation of freedom. Though we may involve ourselves temporarily, in one current event or another, those decisions will be based on the overall foundation, rather than any individual bias. We continually strive to bring together both groups and individuals from a wide spectrum. We seek to unify them to fight for freedom and the preservation of our liberties as a whole.

FOUNDATION

"Unity, not uniformity, must be our aim. We attain unity only through variety. Differences must be integrated, not annihilated, not absorbed." —Mary Parker Follett

Simply stated, the mission of *United in Liberty* is, "To unite freedom-loving patriots in restoring the principles taught by the Founding Fathers both individually (through membership) and collectively (through affiliation with like-minded groups) to activism through education, association, and communication." In its most basic form, the mission statement describes what we are all about. We are organized to unite both individual patriots and freedom-loving groups throughout the country. Our purpose is not just to bring these people and groups together, but to actually affect positive change. We believe the rights vouchsafed by the *Constitution* can and will be preserved in the long run yet we must not wait until they are nearly gone before we fight to preserve them. We believe that in order to see that reality the general public must first, be educated upon the principles of good government and second, be activated in ensuring that such principles are followed. While there are many individuals and groups who are encouraging some of these aspects, we believe that all four pillars must be in place for this type of responsible and true change to occur in the lives of individuals, families, communities and our Country.

As they relate to principles of good government, the four pillars of proper and positive change as are:

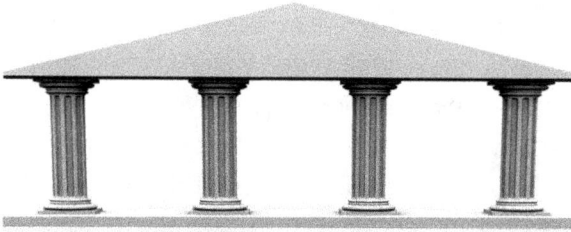

I. *Individuals*   II. *Groups*   III. *Education*   IV. *Activism*

Our motto is **"Saving the Constitution, One Community at a Time."** That is our goal and our daily strive. We aim to ultimately save the principles found in this great document that for so many years has been our foundational rock as a nation. However, we seek to do the saving in a concentrated neighborhood by neighborhood process. The power of *United in Liberty* lies not in its numbers as a whole, but in the strength of individual Community Action Committee groups who meet frequently in their individual regions.

At the core of *United in Liberty* are a set of true principles. A principle is defined as, "A general truth; a law comprehending many subordinate truths," and a "Ground; foundation; that which supports an assertion, an action, or a series of actions or of reasoning" (*Webster's American Dictionary of the English Language*, 1828). In other words, these principles are the very foundation of what we believe. Principles allow a framework or a foundation upon which all action can be measured. The following is a list of what we refer to as *The 12 Principles of Liberty*™ which are the core truthes that will assist us in accomplishing our mission.

THE 12 PRINCIPLES OF LIBERTY™

I. God endows mankind with unalienable rights such as life, liberty and the pursuit of happiness. **(God's Gifts)**

II. Unalienable rights cannot be made, altered or abolished by government or mankind. **(Unalienable Rights)**

III. As its proper role, government is instituted by mankind exclusively to protect unalienable rights. **(Government's Role)**

IV. It is the right of the people to alter or abolish an abusive government. **(Revolution)**

V. All mankind are justified before God in the defense of unalienable rights. **(Defense)**

VI. To ensure freedom, the law must be created by a moral and educated people. **(Morality & Education)**

VII. Freedom can only be sustained through a representative republic. **(Republicanism)**

VIII. To prevent the abuse of power, government must be limited, local, checked and balanced. **(Balanced Government)**

IX. All mankind are created equal before God, the law, and in the protection of their rights. **(Created Equal)**

X. All mankind are created with the ability to choose and each have responsibility for their own agency. **(Agency)**

XI. Prosperity occurs when free enterprise and private property exist with minimal government regulation and restrained debt. **(Prosperity)**

XII. The family, in its traditional form, as ordained by God, is the core unit of free society. **(Family)**

Whenever *United in Liberty* decides to take on a cause, the decision is weighed by each of these principles. No matter how important the cause may seem at the time, if it does not honor one or more of our core principles, we will not become distracted by it. One of our roles is to sit at the back of the boat, to see the overall picture, and to make decisions that will get all of us through the treacherous parts together. The key to success, however, is that we work together. We cannot get involved only when the issues are dearest to our hearts. To be successful, we must unite on all issues of freedom. What does a same-sex marriage law in New York have to do with an anti-homeschool bill in California? In a word, everything! Imagine for a moment, if all of the home school families in California could join with others to fight same-sex marriage in New York. Likewise, imagine that the families affected by the first law in New York, could unite with groups across the nation to help preserve the right to home school in California. We would see a large coalition of freedom loving patriots across the country uniting for the overall preservation of the *Constitution* by fighting as one large country.

Maybe something just happened to your psyche when I mentioned same-sex marriage. "But, I do not believe in that issue," you might protest. "Does that mean I should not be a part of this strength in numbers?" The time for that sort of individualism must end if we are going to be successful as a whole. Just as an individual rafter must put aside their personal agenda at times for the success of the sum total, groups or individuals who love liberty must learn to trust the anchorman and paddle together. If we do not stand to defend the rights of one, who will stand to defend our own?

> *"The feds came for the White Separatists, but I wasn't a White Separatist, so I didn't speak out. They came for the Branch Davidians, but I wasn't a Branch Davidian, so I didn't speak out. They came for the militias, but I wasn't a militia member, so I didn't speak out. They came for the 'assault weapons' owners, but I didn't own any 'assault weapons,' so I didn't speak out. They came for the rest of the gunowners, but I wasn't a gunowner, so I didn't speak out. They came for the holistic health practitioners, the homeschoolers, the ranchers, the Libertarians, the Buchanan Republicans, the Christians, but I*

> *wasn't one of them, so I didn't speak out. Then they came for me, and there was no one left to speak out!"*
> —*(Boston T. Party, back cover of Boston on Guns and Courage).*

Does that mean you will be forced to support a cause that you are not in agreement with? To do so would be a violation of principle. If *United in Liberty* takes on a cause that you feel is in opposition to your morals or ethics, we would not expect you to be involved. In that case, we would encourage you to do nothing. All we ask is that you do become involved in issues that do not violate your personal code of moral values. In return, others will become involved when your particular issues are threatened and together, we will save the *Constitution*.

LIVING BY PRINCIPLE

> *"'Cheshire Puss,' she began, rather timidly, as she did not know at all whether it would like the name: however, it only grinned a little wider. Come, it's pleased so far, thought Alice, and she went on. 'Would you tell me please, which way I ought to go from here?' 'That depends a good deal on where you want to get to,' said the cat. 'I don't much care where,' said Alice. 'Then it doesn't matter which way you go,' said the cat. '... So long as I get somewhere,' Alice added as an explanation. 'Oh, you're sure to do that,' said the cat, 'if you only walk long enough.'" —Lewis Carroll*

A great majority of people would probably fit in one of two categories. Either they are followers or *welldependers*. That does not mean those are the only two categories that one may find themselves in, it simply means that most people are in either one or the other. A follower, by definition, will wait for others to lead out, pick a wagon, and hop on. With regard to major issues, they would leave the hard decisions to someone else. *Welldependers*, on the other hand, are much like a piece of garbage on the high seas. With no power of their own, they become tossed to and fro by every wind or wave which may come upon them. Though they may be in positions which compel them to be decision-makers, they are doing so, based on the situation (and their personal consequences), not upon any founding beliefs

Though we all must make personal decisions, most of them are fairly minor. We must decide what to wear in the morning, which entertainment we will participate in, or what to eat for lunch, for example. More important choices (such as those regarding marriage, family, religion, education, careers, etc.), though less frequent in nature, must also be made. It is probable that most people make life-altering, choices based on circumstance rather than principle as well.

Furthermore, decisions that do not seemingly have a direct effect on our lives (i.e. tax law for the wealthy, who our politicians are, or what is going on in Zimbabwe) we will often leave to others to decide. *If it does not affect me today, I do not care*, appears to be the mantra of the majority. Apathy has replaced patriotism.

There are probably superior, more literate, ways to describe this idea, but they may not be as accurate. *Welldepends* is a personally coined phrase to describe how a majority of decisions are made by many people on a daily basis. It is the opposite of acting on principle. *Welldependers* make choices based on what is expedient rather than what is right.

When a choice is placed before you, how do you decide which one to choose? What makes you take this road versus that? What would happen if you asked a hypothetical question such as, "What would you do if....?" The answer might be, "Well, it depends." Depends on this and depends on that. In other words, the answer depends on the situation.

Here are a few examples for illustration's sake. If you find you are in a situation at work where just a little dishonesty might make you a great deal of money, what would you do? Would the answer depend on your chances of getting caught? Does your choice of whether or not to look at pornography depend on how your spouse feels about it? Does choosing to stand up to and fight to change a bad law depend on whether or not it personally affects your life? If so, you are not living by principle. Rather, you are living by, what we refer to as, 'welldepends.' Such are those who are "Ever learning, and never able to come to the knowledge of the truth" (*KJV* 2 Tim. 3:7).

By definition, principles never change. Ideas are not principles, but there are both productive and unproductive ideas that must be dealt with. For example, if one of your founding ideals is "If it feels good, do it," you may make vastly different choices than one who believes that "God's commandments are absolute." Just because you believe with all of your soul that doing things that make you feel good is correct, does not make it so. Some things are false, even if you believe them to be absolutely true.

Truth is truth. Principles are eternal. As such, they have always existed, do exist presently, and will forever exist without change. Though policies may change, principles are absolute.

Where then does one turn to find these principles? There is one ultimate source, but several distribution centers. Speaking boldly now, all truth comes from God. "...Spirit is truth" (*KJV* 1 John 5:6). Our reception of that truth can and does come in a variety of ways. Those ways may include (but are not limited to), Holy Scripture, Prophets or other spokespersons for Deity, the writings of the Founding Fathers, classical literature, and even direct revelation. The list can continue on as there are countless, as well as various resources available to man.

Despite the fact that principles can be found in a variety of different places, we cannot live by principles if we do not first *know* or understand how to identify them. Thus, one productive idea based in principle is that it is incumbent upon each of us to be proactive in our learning and discover these truths . Once learned, and understood, we are bound by God's law to apply them in directing all other choices.

If truth exists, and it does, why would one need to learn to identify and follow a life of principle? It is best answered by asking what one wishes to accomplish. Remember, it has already been established that the majority of people in this world do not live lives of principle. If you want to be like the majority of people, the need for knowing and living such principles is mute. If, however, you desire to be more than average, principles will lead you in the right direction. Living a life of principle is different than living a life of *welldepends*. While the latter is popular, celebrity does not determine greatness. Living by *welldepends* carries one about by every whim. Life lived on the basis of principle grounds one and makes every decision more lucid.

When one makes a conscious decision to live by principle, each decision made from that point on becomes rooted in what is right, rather than what is easy, popular, pleasurable, or prudent. Grounded in principle, decisions are made based on one criteria—what is right!

How does this look to the untrained eye? The formula is three-fold. First, one must decide, as the old Johnny Cash song asks, "What is Truth?" This may indeed be the most difficult step for some. It requires study, prayer, and learning to listen to the Spirit. For those who are untrained in this process, the learning curve may take some time.

Second, simple yet firm principles must be established. Decide, based on truth, what principles you will live by. The format for these declarations can be varied, but should be short, defined declarations of truth. Examples may include, "Honesty is always the best policy," or "God is the author of life," or "...all men are created equal, [and] are endowed by their Creator with certain unalienable rights..." (*Declaration of Independence*).

The final, and most important step to living a life of principle is to SLOW DOWN and make deliberate decisions based on these truths. This too can be a difficult step for those who are not used to living in this manner. It requires a conscious commitment to think before a decision is made. In a world of split-second verdicts, this part takes practice. Ask yourself which principle the decision adheres to or if a principle is being violated. If you have not yet discovered a principle for a particular situation, you may begin to identify one based upon another principle that you *have* discovered. Remember, you must not make your decision based on what you perceive the outcome will be. Make the decision based on principles and upon principles only. As you do so, you will always be able to support your decision as predicated on sound doctrine.

From seemingly insignificant choices, such as how to dress or what to eat to more momentous decisions such as family planning or religious affiliation, we are constantly deciding the fate of our lives. Most would leave those choices to chance or expediency. There is a better way. When we view our lives from an eternal perspective, true principles will naturally follow.

Yes, the large majority of people are either followers or *welldepend-ers*. When faced with a choice and asked what we will do, our answer ought to be, "Well, it depends on which principle is involved here."

GOVERNMENT AT IT'S MOST BASIC LEVEL

"These wards, called townships in New England, are the vital principles of their governments and have proved themselves the wisest invention ever devised by the wit of man for the perfect exercise of self-government, and for its preservation" —Thomas Jefferson

At the time the Children of Israel left for the Promised Land, Moses found himself overwhelmed with the burdens of being a leader. His Father-in-Law, Jethro, gave Moses some sound advice. "Moreover thou shalt provide out of all the people able men, such as fear God, men of truth, hating covetousness; and place such over them, to be rulers of thousands, and rulers of hundreds, rulers of fifties, and rulers of tens: And…they shall bear the burden with thee" (*KJV* Exodus 18:21-22). Though Moses was a great leader and understood the importance of his calling, it was Jethro who taught the principle which made it all work. One man could not and should not do it all himself. By dividing the group into smaller, yet united groups, they were having a greater affect on the population as a whole than they could have otherwise. The Founders understood this law and America was organized in a similar fashion. Though there was a central, federal government, there

"...the way to have good and safe government, is not to trust it all to one, but to divide it among the many, distributing to every one

exactly the functions he is competent to. Let the national government be entrusted with the defense of the nation, and its foreign and federal relations; the State governments with the civil rights, laws, police, and administration of what concerns the State generally; the counties with the local concerns of the counties, and each ward direct the interests within itself. It is by dividing and subdividing these republics from the great national one down through all its subordinations, until it ends in the administration of every man's farm by himself; by placing under every one what his own eye may superintend, that all will be done for the best. What has destroyed liberty and the rights of man in every government which has ever existed under the sun? The generalizing and concentrating all cares and power into one body...Where every man is a sharer in the direction of his ward-republic, or of some of the higher ones, and feels that he is a participator in the government of affairs, not merely at an election one day in the year, but every day."

—Thomas Jefferson

were also States, Counties, Districts, Townships/Wards, etc.

The Founders were students of history. History had established (whether for ill in Russia and France or good in Ancient Israel), government works best when run at the smallest, most local level. Though we have strayed (or completely forsaken) ourselves from that principle, it is as true today as it was for the Children of Israel. Correct principles are such, whether or not we choose to adhere to them and they do not change with time.

If we are going to affect change in this country, we must return to our roots. We must rise up and cause change in our states, our counties, our towns, our school districts, our neighborhoods, and especially in our own family and individual lives. It will never work from the top down. It must come from the most common denominator and work its way up.

THE PARABLE OF THE LIONS

"Government big enough to supply everything you need is big

enough to take everything you have ... The course of history shows that as a government grows, liberty decreases."
—*Thomas Jefferson*

There once was a pride of lions and within the society were many diverse lions. There were male lions with large, flowing manes and female lions with short, comely coats. There were several wise and experienced lions and they were mingled with the younger, more energetic, yet—naïve. Overall, the lion pride was functioning as it should, most were happy, at least they thought they were. Despite the normal appearance of the lion community, there seemed to be something slightly wrong. It was not something tangible that could be seen, heard, or touched. No, it was just a small, almost imperceptible gnawing on the psyche.

Due to the size of the pride, it had been decided many years previous that there must be a ruling body. Some had fought against this organization because, after all, lions are rulers. *How ridiculous that rulers should need rulers of their own.* Nevertheless, the majority could see the *wisdom* of organization and it was done. For many years, the governing bodies worked well. They built hunting paths through the jungle. They dug centralized dens for group meetings. They solved disputes between lion families. Overall, they did much and they did it under the banner of *good for the whole.*

After a fair amount of time, things began to change...but only a little. Though the leading body continued to do what was *best for the pride*, some individual lions began to feel threatened. A few families had much of their spoils taken from them and given to families who had less. Lions with *authority* would sometimes come to the homes of lion families unannounced and search their dens for unauthorized objects. Closed-den agreements were being made with monkeys, elephants, and even other lion prides in order to be seen as forging relationships with *all jungle-kind*. In all, freedoms and liberties were being sacrificed, but only a little and only for the good of the whole. At least, that was the mantra.

An outsider looking in might believe that all was well. The lion pride appeared to be prosperous and flourishing. Not until one spoke candidly to certain families would certain bitterness be revealed. Furthermore, not even a large majority of lions felt disenfranchised. Many—mostly receivers of the benefits—did not want things to change at all.

Oh, there were some concerned pockets. Some lions were studying history and learning that things had not always been this way. Others were talking to their neighbors and trying to get others involved, but not having much success. Still others were concentrated on the secrets and *conspiracy theories*. They seemed to be so wrapped up and concerned with things, that they could not do anything about these issues they could have an effect on. There was uneasiness alright, but things were not changing very quickly.

One day, things did change. Something happened that did not transform everything, but it did alter them. It certainly gave justification for the governing bodies to continue their usurpations of power. On a Friday morning in the spring, a young lion who had recently lost his position within the pride, killed 13 of *his own kind* with his paw. Sliced them to bits.

Not three hours later, the leaders of the pride were in front of the cameras. "Something must be done," was their rhetoric. "It was not his fault. He should have never been allowed to have claws in the first place. Surely, the desperate situation of the economy, his recent job loss, and the fact that he had no health care benefits has caused him to do this!"

The emotion of the situation was hard for anyone to ignore. Even some of the old-timers were persuaded that things needed to be changed. Laws must be passed…for the good of the whole. It was moved that all lions should have their claws removed immediately. There were still some, though not large in numbers, who kept their heads about themselves. "Don't you understand? When you give up freedom for safety, you lose both," they cried.

It was those few patriots who gathered together and started a movement. At first, the faction could not be accurately described as a *movement*. Just a few lions here and a few lions there. They began to educate themselves. They read books and biographies by the founding lions of the pride. As they read, they began to understand just how removed the pride had become from the principles which were espoused in the very beginning. Once that was realized, it was only natural that a restoration these ideologies was strongly desired. They began to meet with other—like minded—lions. It soon became obvious that there were more than just a few lions who felt as they did. Most of them, before now, had remained in the shadows. The groups were purposefully kept small, thus allowing discussion from all, yet they had cross-affiliation with many other small groups of the entire pride. Each was doing things to affect policies at the most local of levels. Numbers were being gathered to influence local policies. Lions within the small groups—who believed in these principles—were volunteering, running, and winning elections. The small things were turning into larger things and their effect was soon felt on a much broader basis. Though the lion elite fought against the group, the sheer numbers of lion patriots were overwhelming to them. Because they had not waited until they had lost their Representative Republic Pride completely, they were able to work within the system to restore the system. Though there were hurdles along the way, the project was a tremendous success. After a long time, freedom and liberty were restored to the lion pride.

Much like the Lion Parable, I believe in the patriots of this nation. I know a majority of Americans still believe in the principles espoused by the Founding Fathers. Yes, I did say a *Majority*. Though it may not seem that way when you look around and notice what is happening to our Republic, I am convinced that deep in the heart of most Americans, they know what is right and they know what is wrong. The reason we are losing our liberties is not because we do not know the problem. The reason we are losing our freedom is two-fold; we are either lazy, ignorant, —or both.

LAZINESS AND IGNORANCE

"If a man takes no interest in public affairs, we do not commend

him as quiet but condemn him as useless." —Thucydides

Politics is a funny topic with most people. Too many of us have taken to heart the ill-conceived advice of our mothers to "never talk about religion or politics in public." Perhaps the reason for the advice is that these two topics are so full of raw emotion for most people. Perhaps we are to be docile and never bring up topics that will enflame or excite those we speak to. To do so might hurt feelings and change relationships., but possibly, it may be wise to take that chance in some cases.

Lazy people are what they are, but they can change. We let too many good things get in the way of better things. We must determine what is most important and place our best efforts there. Funny thing about time; God blessed all with the same amount. Black or white, bond or free, rich or poor—we all have 24 hours per day to accomplish whatever it is we decide to accomplish. When that day does come, and we meet the Founding Fathers face to face, and they ask, "What have you done with the freedom we pledged our lives, our fortunes, our families and our sacred honor for?" The excuse of "My favorite television show was on," will probably not cut it.

Next, the ignoramus. This word is not meant to be a offensive. Though it has been used by some to cause offense, the purest meaning of the word is not distasteful. Webster defines the ignorant as "A person untaught or uninformed" (Webster, 1828). Frankly, we are all ignorant in many things. We simply cannot know all things. We may pretend to know something about everything, but in the end, we are all ignorant to a degree. Ignorance is caused by omitting—whether purposefully or passively—study of the topic we are ignorant of. There is one solution to ignorance—education. That education can come though personal study, formal classes, or discussion with others. No matter how the education comes, when it does come, you will feel a swelling within to do something about the knowledge you now possess. Once you learn true principles and plant them in your hearts, you may then notice those around you are not living by them. Suddenly, you will have an unquenchable desire to do something. You may even feel as if you want to save the world.

Saving the world is a daunting task, but as the proverbial saying goes, so is eating an elephant. Maybe that is why most of us never even try. With the proper structure, however, it is possible—one bite at a time. Perhaps you are finding people who, like you, are frustrated with the current events taking place in our government or communities. People who, like you, want to do something, but do not know where to or even how to begin. "How can I possibly change Washington?" they ask. Well, it can certainly be done and the time to start is never more important than now. It will take a concerted and deliberate effort for it to occur. For this to be effective it must begin at the most grassroots of levels, within your minds, then family, then community followed by the nation, but it can be done.

WHAT WILL IT TAKE?

> *"Of course, the first step to improvement and reform is education. The next step is action. The principles of the Constitution were not meant only to be studied, but to be restored and put into full operation. Much of this could be done now."* —Dr. W. Cleon Skousen

In order for *United in Liberty* to be effective in this effort, certain elements must be in place. At the core, its members must be studying. Self-education is essential for success. Oliver Wendell Holmes said, "Man's mind, once stretched by a new idea, never regains its original dimensions." That education must be combined with affiliation with other like-minded individuals in small-group settings. These groups must commit to meet regularly and, not only share what they are learning on their own, but discuss local issues that are destroying freedoms and decide together what they will do about it. These groups are constantly seeking converts from among their family, friends, neighbors, etc. As they grow in numbers, they grow in influence. Some will seek for public office. With the support of their fellows, they will win and begin to affect change from the *inside*. Small group leaders will meet semi-regularly with other group leaders in regional settings. It is there that ideas will be shared within groups. Direction will be given from the national center (the anchorman) and these small groups will unite on common goals. Tyranny will erode and freedom will grow across this great Nation.

The other leg of our success rests on our willingness to be inclusive. We understand that there are worthy groups with honorable projects. Instead of being exclusionary, we are inviting all. The only requirement we insist upon is that you agree with our mission statement and a majority of the principles we hold as sacred. If your group fits in this category, we invite you to join us. Affiliation together, will bring about change for your projects and ours.

United in Liberty is effective because it caters to all freedom-loving patriots. To the patriotic groups across this nation (large and small) we say, keep fighting for your specific and choice projects, and now join with us. Let us fight the battles together. Together, we can restore our lost freedoms and liberties while we are ***"Saving the Constitution, One Community at a Time."***

CHAPTER II

❧

God endows mankind with unalienable rights such as life, liberty and the pursuit of happiness.

"Life, faculties, production—in other words individuality, liberty, property—this is man. And in spite of the cunning of artful political leaders, these three gifts from God proceed all human legislation, and are superior to it." —Frederic Bastiat

INTRODUCTION

"Facts are stubborn things," —John Adams

Truth is truth whether or not one chooses to believe it or—even more—embrace it. If you have two objects and add another two, you have four objects. This is a matter of fact. You can say it isn't so. You can discredit the individual describing the math problem using ad hominem. Out of ignorance or malice, you can teach the answer is six. Any of these reactions does not change the reality. A disbelief in the law of gravity does not change its eternal existence. The truth is—God exists. He is a loving Heavenly Father, who because of His love for us and desire for each us to succeed, has given us certain gifts. Among these gifts are the right to life, the right to liberty, and the right to pursue a course leading to happiness.

One can choose not to believe in God. Others might acknowledge His influence, but call Him "Nature" (or something other than what He is). One has the liberty to do so. What one chooses to believe regarding Him, or what one chooses to call Him, does not change or alter the principle. Furthermore, what one believes regarding God or his or her own faith should not determine whether or not he or she understands this principle. Simply stated, if you believe you have the right to live, be free, and follow your dreams, you are a believer in this truth.

THE FOUNDERS WERE GOD-FEARING MEN

"One of the most astonishing aspects of the American historical development is the providential manner in which the right people were at the right place and inspired at the right time to do the right things." —Dr. W. Cleon Skousen

Truth: most, of the Founding Fathers of this Nation were believers in God. There has been a movement over the past several decades to paint these men as unethical, immoral, dishonest, reprobates. Though some would strive to discredit these men, exploit their weaknesses, and generally paint them in a negative light, the truth was quite the opposite. Much of the negative reporting on their beliefs stems more from their wariness of organized religion and downright fear of religious zealots rather than a disbelief in God Himself. In studying their writings, one finds that most pronounced a firm and steadfast belief in God. This does not mean to say they were perfect men. They were still men and, had their weaknesses. You have probably heard some of the stories regarding their morality. In the end, however, they were men inspired of God to perform the tasks given them and could not have been if they had been exceedingly unrighteous.

John Adams was a man of character, purpose, and duty. He had a deep love and eternal commitment to his wife, Abigail and his children. He has, at times, been chided by historians for the time spent away from them, but none of us can know his heart. We know not his divine mission in life and where the Lord directed his efforts.

Benjamin Franklin, often painted by the opposition as a womanizing reprobate, was a man of deep faith and a strong believer in prayer. It was Franklin, who at an impasse during the Constitutional Convention of 1787, suggested that the delegates ought to open with prayer each day and invoke the name of Him under whose authority they actually met.

Alexander Hamilton was never an old man. He died before he was fifty from wounds suffered in a duel with a political foe. Throughout his life and again on his death bed, he proclaimed a love for and a desire to gain mercy from his Savior.

The Father of our *Constitution*, James Madison, was vocal in his giving credit to the One who actually wrote it. Yet, there are those who would now have us take the Ten Commandments off of public buildings, remove *'In God We Trust'* from coinage, and strike *'One nation under God'* from our pledge, despite the honorable men who put them there in the first place.

Most of the negative quotes regarding the Founders and their religious ideals come from the writings of Thomas Jefferson. Jefferson was not a non-believer, however. He was a man of history. He had read and studied much of ancient and modern civilizations. He had knowledge of how the zeal of religion could impair a worship of God. His attacks on religion should not be confused with his belief in God. And even Thomas Paine, accused atheist, acknowledged his belief in God at times.

Finally we look to the great leader of the Revolution and Father of our Country, George Washington. It is he who, as the Patriarch of our Nation, was unabashed in his outspoken praise to the Almighty. He invoked His name boldly and frequently in his speeches to the nation.

It is interesting to note that when Washington took the oath of office as our first President, he added four words that many today believe to just be a part of the original text. A reading of Article Two, Section One, Clause Eight of the *Constitution* reveals none such. The words were "So Help Me God." When he had said them, he bent and kissed the Bible.

From Their Own Christian Lips

*"The general principles upon which the Fathers achieved indepen-
dence were the general principals of Christianity... I will avow that I
believed and now believe that those general principles of Christianity
are as eternal and immutable as the existence and attributes of God."*
— John Adams

*"Here is my creed: I believe in one God, the Creator of the universe.
That he governs it by his providence. That he ought to be worshipped.
That the most acceptable service we render to him is in doing good to
his other children...As to Jesus of Nazareth, my Opinion of whom you
particularly desire, I think the System of Morals and his Religion, as
he left them to us, is the best the World ever saw, or is likely to see."*
— Benjamin Franklin

*"I have a tender reliance on the mercy of the Almighty, through the
merits of the Lord Jesus Christ. I am a sinner. I look to Him for
mercy; pray for me."*
— Alexander Hamilton

*"We've staked our future on our ability to follow the Ten Command-
ments with all of our heart. We have staked the whole future of
American civilization, not upon the power of government, far from
it. We've staked the future of all our political institutions upon our
capacity...to sustain ourselves according to the Ten Commandments
of God."*
— James Madison

*"My views...are the result of a life of inquiry and reflection, and very
different from the anti-Christian system imputed to me by those who
know nothing of my opinions. To the corruptions of Christianity I
am, indeed, opposed; but not to the genuine precepts of Jesus himself.*

I am a Christian in the only sense in which He wished any one to be; sincerely attached to his doctrines in preference to all others."

— Thomas Jefferson

"I believe in one God, and no more and I hope for happiness beyond this life"

— Thomas Paine

"The name of American, which belongs to you, in your national capacity, must always exalt the just pride of Patriotism, more than any appellation derived from local discriminations. With slight shades of difference, you have the same religion...reason and experience both forbid us to expect, that national morality can prevail in exclusion of religious principle."

— George Washington

MANIFEST DESTINY

"It has been the will of Heaven that we should be thrown into existence at a period when the greatest philosophers and law-givers of antiquity would have wished to live ... a period when a coincidence of circumstances without example has afforded to thirteen colonies at once an opportunity of beginning government anew from the foundation and building as they choose. How few of the human race have ever had an opportunity of choosing a system of government for themselves and their children? How few have ever had anything more of choice in government than in climate?" —John Adams

The term *Manifest Destiny* is often cited in reference to the expansion of the United States to the Western frontier (From Sea to Shining Sea) in the 1800's. This reference is accurate. The Founders saw a slightly different *Manifest Destiny* for the ultimate future of this nation. In their eyes, America and her governmental form were forged by the grace of the Almighty Himself. They seemed to see His hand in all that they were doing and in its eventual prospect. This belief was not some mystic notion conjured up in their minds. They believed it wholeheartedly as they were living through the beginning stages of it. Not only had God seen them through the overwhelming odds of the Revolution, but He would continue to guide and prosper them far into the future.

Fifty-five men, some farmers, some merchants, some lawyers, some statesmen. Different backgrounds, different politics, different family makeup. Some wealthy, some deeply in debt, but most of moderate means. Twelve States, some agricultural, some industrious which had varying ideas of what should be done and how it was to be accomplished. They came for the *sole and express purpose of revising the Articles of Confederation*, yet from that event a new government, and new nation was born.

George Washington was probably the first of the Founders to use the word, *Miracle* in regard to this great work. But truly, they all felt that they were inspired from on High as they framed the Government of the United States. That government, the first of its kind, would stand alone as a beacon of freedom to the world for hundreds of years to come. Surely, the Founders did not see the Revolution, the founding documents, and the establishment of a new government as a simple *flash in the pan*.

There has even been much allegory applied between the Children of Israel of Moses' time and the Colonists of General Washington's. An honest student of American history will freely acknowledge the Lord's Almighty hand in its formation. Here were a few, mostly untrained, *rag-tag* patriots fighting what, at the time, was the world's super power. Surely the revolution would not have succeeded without His divine intervention. Further, with the amount of discord and political dissidence in that hallowed hall in Philadelphia, the document that has stood for over two-hundred years could not have been formed without His authorship. America was His doing and this, indeed, is His promised land.

Any casual look at history will reveal the Lord's hand in the founding and destiny of this country. The men gathered at this time in history, with the backgrounds and visions they brought to the table, and the miracle that was the *Declaration of Independence*, Revolution, and capstone of the Constitutional Convention was no mistake. This is God's Country and it is He who will decide its fate based upon our level of righteousness.

ENDOWMENTS GIVEN/RIGHTS ARE FREE

"An important test I use in passing judgment upon an act of government is this: If it were up to me as an individual to punish my neighbor for violating a given law, would it offend my conscience to do so?"

—*Ezra Taft Benson*

An Endowment in its most basic description, is simply a gift. By its very nature, a gift cannot be earned. If a gift is earned, it then ceases to be a gift and instead becomes a reward or payment. Thus, you cannot do anything in mortality to earn your life, your freedom or your ability to prosper. Those rights are given to you—freely—from God.

This simple declaration may cause some to dispute. One might argue that the cancer patient is fighting for his or her life. One could opine that the slave may fight for his freedom. One may believe that the capitalist is constantly fighting for his right to succeed and be happy. Each of these statements would be right. You can and should, fight for each of these if they are under attack. However, fighting for these elements is different than creating them. They, as rights, are already there. Indeed they are gifts from God given freely to each man. All men who walk on this earth are entitled to life, liberty, and the pursuit of happiness. One might look on the concentration camp prisoner and say, "They have no happiness, liberty, or much of a life." Though probably accurate, they still have the *right* to them. At the present time, those rights are likely being denied. The term 'probably' is used because there may be exceptions. Victor Frankl taught, that even in a concentration camp, it is possible to pursue happiness because these are gifts from God, those who strive to take away any of these rights cannot escape the consequences that inevitably will follow.

Are these the only gifts given to mankind from God? No. When Jefferson penned the *Declaration of Independence*, he wrote, "...all men are created equal, that they are endowed by their Creator with certain unalienable Rights, that *among these* are Life, Liberty, and the pursuit of happiness" (*Declaration of Independence*, emphasis added). By choosing the phrase, "among these," he implied that there are also others.

> "Let us identify some of the unalienable rights or natural rights which the Founders knew existed but did not enumerate in the Declaration of Independence: The right of self-government. The right to bear arms for self-defense. The right to own, develop, and dispose of property. The right to make personal choices. The right of free conscience. The right to choose a profession. The right to choose a mate. The right to beget one's kind. The right to assemble. The right to petition. The right to free speech. The right to a free press. The right to enjoy the fruits of one's labors. The right to improve one's position through barter and sale. The right to contrive and invent. The right to explore the natural resources of the earth. The right to privacy. The right to provide personal security. The right to provide nature's necessities—air, food, water, clothing, and shelter. The right to a fair trial. The right of free association. The right to contract"
>
> –Dr. W. Cleon Skousen

There, undoubtedly are others. It was not a mistake that Jefferson chose to pen just three—life, liberty, and the pursuit of happiness. It is these three that form the umbrella for all others. Indeed, each of the 22 rights recited by Dr. Skousen could be placed on the same foundation as the three grand human rights. The right of self-government, for example, is simply a subset of the right to liberty. The right to bear arms for self-defense relates to the right to life. The right to own, develop, and dispose of property is another way of referring to the right to the pursuit of happiness. The right to make personal choices could arguably relate to all three. And so it goes. There is not a God-given right that would not fit under the umbrella of the three original rights.

It is here that one must be careful to not take too much liberty. It has become the nature of political activists to use the word *right* to refer to just about any privilege one can imagine. It has now become popular to speak of the right to get an abortion, the right to a clean environment, the right to welfare assistance, or the right for everyone to receive a free education as *unalienable rights*. There is one, simple problem with these rights; that is, they are not rights at all.

If a law has no basis in natural right, it has no basis at all. There is a simple formula that can be used to identify whether or not a proposed (or current) law is a *right* or simply someone's bright idea of something that should be a right. The test is to ask oneself if you feel morally justified in punishing your neighbors if they were to violate that particular law. For example, would you feel right about demanding and enforcing your rich neighbor to give up 20% of his income to your poor neighbor? One's conscience will never allow one to feel good about something that is inherently wrong. If you would not do it yourself, you cannot permit your people-authorized government to do it. Government, after all, is simply a bigger *gang*. When one applies such logic to any governmental or social program, it is quite easy to sift the wheat from the tares.

THE RIGHT TO LIFE

> *"[Self-defense is] the primary law of nature [which cannot be] taken away by the law of society." —William Blackstone*

The most fundamental of all human rights is that to life and the protection of such. It is a right which precedes legislation, government, customs, and civilization. Unless he has committed a wrong which removes that fundamental principle, man has a right to life.

It is for this reason that the act of aborting a baby is a violation of principle. Pro-choicers would claim the right to liberty or the right to the pursuit of happiness is trampled when their right to choose an abortion is denied. Though that may technically seem accurate, the right to life (the life of the baby) trumps both the right to liberty and the pursuit of happiness.

The only justification for impeding the freedoms of another is to prevent harm to himself or those around him. Over one's own body (or in the protection of those among him) is an absolute sovereign fundamental. When the Founders spoke of unalienable rights, they nearly always listed life first. This was no mistake. Thus, two laws must be prioritized with *Natural Law*: First comes the protection of life, and second liberty and the freedom to pursue prosperity.

There are some who would try to use the right to life to justify the violation of principle. The debate over government-run universal health-care is an example. Proponents would say, "We have a right to life and health, affects that right. Thus, we have a right to free health care." There are many problems with that statement beginning with the fact that nothing (especially a government-run program) is free. It is important to first understand that the debate over *universal health-care* is not a contest over health *care* at all. It is a question over whether or not tax-payers should be liable for the *payment* of such health-care. In other words, it is an argument over who should pay! No one would dispute the fact that it is one's moral obligation to render help where needed. Christ taught that lesson well with the parable of the Good Samaritan (*KJV* Luke 10:25-37). However, one would have a hard time convincing others that one has a *legal* responsibility to do so. No major hospital would turn an ailing man away at the door for lack of ability to pay. Should the cost of his treatment be passed on to the tax-payer? The answer to that question does not concern the principle of a right to life. Again, the medical assistance would be provided and the cost of that assistance is another question all-together.

THE RIGHT TO LIBERTY

"Under the law of nature, all men are born free, every one comes into the world with a right to his own person, which includes the

liberty of moving and using it at his own will. This is what is called personal liberty, and is given him by the Author"
—*Thomas Jefferson*

More wars have been fought over the right to liberty than for any other reason; whether they be *holy* wars, revolutions, or *civil* wars. Even wars over land and territories are essentially wars of freedom. When the freedom of a people has been denied for an extended period of time, the hearts of the people will eventually rebel, and unless the oppressors relent, blood will ultimately be shed.

The right to liberty is what caused the Children of Israel to leave Egypt and travel into a desolate and unknown territory. It is the reason the Crusades and both World Wars were fought. Even our own country, fought wars on our own soil over freedom.

Deeply ingrained in the human soul is the desire to be free. One must be free to make decisions, travel, work, play, buy goods, marry, have children, and live life to the fullest. Liberty, in its most basic form, is the right to do anything one pleases, as long as what he is doing does not hurt or impede the rights of those around him. Simply put, if your liberty does not step on the natural rights of others, it is just. That definition is very broad, yet very limited. If that litmus test were applied by politicians consistently, our country may look quite different today.

THE RIGHT TO THE PURSUIT OF HAPPINESS

"A right to happiness doesn't, for me, make much more sense than a right to be six feet tall, or to have a millionaire for your father, or to get good weather whenever you want to have a picnic"
—*C.S. Lewis*

Many people today might equate the pursuit of happiness to the pursuit of pleasure. The Founders did not, they understood the difference. The Nation's Fathers were highly educated and studied much of the ancient philosophers. One philosopher often read and quoted by our Founding Fathers was Aristotle. In *Nicomachean Eth-*

ics, he describes in detail, the *good life*. It is being in tune with our moral compass. It is to know and live the virtues implanted in us by the Creator. Indeed the closer one lives to the will of God, the more happiness one feels. The better one comprehends and lives His will, the more joy one receives. "For the life of the man who is active in accordance with virtue will be happy" (*Nichomachean Ethics Book X*).

The laws of Nature are clear. One must be able to chase such happiness, but arriving is forever the unknown factor. Surely, happiness is more than a destination and Aristotle understood this. The Founders understood this as well. Notice, Jefferson did not write, "...that among these are life, liberty, a*nd happiness*." There is no right to happiness, only a Natural Right for the freedom to *pursue* happiness. Indeed, it is in the active pursuit of a better life that one is truly happy. It is in the dream, in the development, in the risk, in the achievement and yes, it is even in the failure, for only through falling can one experience the true joy of succeeding.

So how does one *pursue* happiness, and why is that right the one the Founder's felt inclined to specifically protect? Though the pursuit of happiness is an individual right that has no boundaries, the realization of such is almost exclusively American. Dr. Oliver Van DeMille, of George Wythe College, describes the "American Way" as being based on five, main pillars upon which the Founders lived. They include: 1) Georgics - the principle of being self-reliant. 2) Providence - relying on a higher power. 3) Liber - education which will lead to one's mission in life. 4) Public Virtue- sacrificing for the good of society, and 5) Freedom. Of the five, all of which allow one to *pursuit happiness*, only one—Freedom, is still held in high regard in this country. Currently, this pillar is also in grave danger of being lost (*The Four Lost American Ideals*, audio CD).

Indeed, the Founding Fathers were about achieving the American Dream, but not in the sense that we now think of it. They believed in the American Dream as it was originally conceived. One must be free to live life to the fullest. Though not all will choose the path of entrepreneurialism, education, seeking their mission in life, and ultimately prosperity; each must be free to do so. The American Dream must be thought of, not in terms of scarcity, but in terms of abundance. It is a better life for all, with the opportunity for success afforded to each and the ability to achieve the highest position to which one is able regardless of the conditions of their birth (James Truslow Adams, *The Epic of America*).

The term used by Abraham Maslow was self-actualization. He defines self-actualization to be "the desire for self-fulfillment, namely the tendency for him to become actualized in what he is potentially. This tendency might be phrased as the desire to become more and more what one is, to become everything that one is capable of becoming."

In the Founder's America, each individual was valuable, each had great potential, each should remain free to reach that potential. Ultimately, it was the government's primary purpose to protect any encroachment upon these, essential rights. Indeed, this is the ultimate purpose of government establishments.

HAPPINESS - SYNONYMOUS WITH PROPERTY

"The purpose of government is the greatest quantity of human happiness." —John Adams

It seems clear that when Jefferson was writing the *Declaration of Independence*, he was likely drawing heavily upon John Locke. Locke combined the words Life, Liberty, and Property, in his essays on government. It is unknown why Jefferson chose to use the phrase, "the pursuit of happiness," instead of the word property. Possibly, it was to help guard against the federal government, at some future time, giving away free land (though that is exactly what they did during the Homestead Act of 1862), to citizens. Possibly, it was to use a phrase which was more encompassing than just property (for *the pursuit of happiness* obviously includes *property*, but also means much more). In the end, the answer to this question is not important.

When one reads the founding documents, it is obvious even to the casual observer, that the terms *pursuit of happiness*, and *property*, are often used seemingly interchangeably. Most of the time, when the *right to the pursuit of happiness* is spoken of, the *right to property* could be substituted and the sentence would have essentially, the same meaning.

George Mason, in writing the first article of the Virginia Declaration of Rights (which was highly influential in Jefferson's drafting of the United States *Declaration of Independence*) wrote, "That all men are by nature equally free and independent, and have certain inherent rights, of which, when they enter into a state of society, they cannot, by any compact, deprive or divest their posterity; namely, the enjoyment of life and liberty, with the means of acquiring and possessing property, and pursuing and obtaining happiness and safety."

CONCLUSION

"…The right to his life, the right to his liberty, the right to his property. The three great rights are so bound together as to be essentially one right." —George Sutherland

"Life, Liberty, and the Pursuit of Happiness," it is likely the most famous phrase in all of the founding documents—perhaps in all of history. It is upon these three great pillars that freedom rests.

Locke taught that man is born with natural privileges. He is also born with the power to protect and preserve those rights—specifically life, liberty, and estate. If he imposes his rights to improperly take the liberties of others, he then is subject to punishment, not shy of including the stripping of his own rights.

It is only in the protection of such that government is justified. In a free society, these rights cannot be denied, unequally distributed nor separated. To strip man of one, is to strip man of all.

CHAPTER III

※·⋇

Unalienable rights cannot be made, altered or abolished by government or mankind.

"The sacred rights of mankind are not to be rummaged for, among old parchments, or musty records. They are written, as with a sunbeam, in the whole volume of human nature, by the hand of the divinity itself; and can never be erased or obscured by mortal power." —Alexander Hamilton

INTRODUCTION

"Rights are not gifts from one man to another, nor from one class of men to another....It is impossible to discover any origin of rights otherwise than in the origins of man; it consequently follows that rights appertain to man in right of his existence, and must therefore be equal to every man." —Thomas Paine

Within the minds of men lies the conflicting belief which, if left unchecked, leads to a life lived not by principle, but rather a life lived by emotion and chance. For centuries, individuals have grappled between the ideas of whether rights are granted by governments and the institutions of men are of Divine origin. These ideas leave individuals torn regarding their preservation and safekeeping. If the choice an individual makes pulls them from that of the Divine, only to rely upon the faculties of men as the so-called guardians of their freedom, it is only after a great deal of struggle and strife that man must eventually demand the speedy return to the Hand of Providence. For that freedom and liberty which men once sought to control, provides truth and light to the mind, and the moral code by which they must live.

We need to first understand the source of these rights so we can comprehend their very nature as they apply to life on an individual and collective basis. When one begins to acknowledge the reality of this primary truth, the desire to protect what was bestowed upon all men becomes paramount to all else. For who would stand idly by and watch the rights of their brother trampled underfoot and not rush to his aid?

The origin of these rights is most important in their preservation and application. Once this discovery is made, the conscience will confirm its Divine truth and nothing will stand in the way of their protection.

At every turn, the enemies of freedom, liberty and personal accountability lie in wait to add the unaware and uninformed to their ranks. These destroyers of freedom are consistent in lying the sandy foundation of false dogma. The fight against such is the only governmental preservation, support and sustenance for which we should concern ourselves.

NATURAL LAW AS THE SOURCE

"Under the law of nature, all men are born free, every one comes into the world with a right to his own person, which includes the liberty of moving and using it at his own will. This is what is called personal liberty, and is given him by the Author of nature, because necessary for his own sustenance." —Thomas Jefferson

With every individual, there inevitably comes an important choice to make regarding how they will live their life. First, one can choose to be deceived by refusing to take accountability for their individual learning, crippling themselves in the very process. Second, an individual can choose to become a deceiver, knowing the truth, but seeking to rob the agency and accountability of another. By so doing, they cripple the mind of their brother and make him a serf to those using intellect.

As unalienable rights are neither granted by government, nor are they bestowed by any institution set up by men, it is beyond reason to think these institutions can create, grant, or withdraw unalienable rights under any condition or circumstance. The source of these rights is nothing less than Divine in nature and this Eternal source is the only true promise of their preservation. Our *Declaration of Independence* states plainly in its opening and closing statements from whence these rights have come, "...the separate and equal station to which the Laws of Nature and of Nature's God entitle them," and later, "... and for the support of this Declaration, with a firm reliance on the protection of Divine Providence..."

Recorded among our founding documents are clear and unmistakable confessions appertaining to that which each of the Framers of this great nation clearly understood to be just and true. Regarded as self-evident, these rights are afforded to all men, irrespective of cultural or ethnic background, educational upbringing and/or material circumstance. In the forming and writing of the *Declaration of Independence*, Jefferson did not seek to ask the British crown for acceptance in living or holding to the rights as outlined. Rather, he simply pointed out the moral code by which he and those assembled with him had chosen to live. It must also be noted that, had Jefferson and those with him not drawn a clear line in their Declaration of Principles, it would not alter the reality, significance, or source of these rights endowed to men. Again, some things are true regardless of our acknowledgement of them.

As Principle #1 illustrates, 'God endows mankind with unalienable rights...' it is to be understood that an individual's denial of the existence of a Supreme Being, Creator or any form of the Divine, will not alter the validity of, nor change the reality of these rights. They exist, and in their very existence they apply to all men. To quote William Shakespeare, "Truth is Truth. To the end of reckoning."

WHAT IS UNALIENABLE?

"Those rights, then, which God and nature have established, and are therefore called natural rights, such as life and liberty, need not the aid of human laws to be more effectually invested in every man than they are; neither do they receive any additional strength when declared by the municipal laws to be inviolate. On the contrary, no human legislature has power to abridge or destroy them, unless the owner shall himself commit some act that amounts to a forfeiture." —William Blackstone

Unalienable. It is a word we toss around when talking about our rights, but do we ever pause to think about what it actually means? To start, let's break it down. 'Un' is not. Alien means foreign, and able is a word with the connotation to make. Put these together and you get a word describing something that cannot be made foreign. In other words, it is something which is part of who we are naturally, and cannot be alienated from us. Webster defines the word Unalienable as "that may not be transferred" (1828).

The phrase *unalienable rights*, *natural rights*, or *law of nature* are used by the Founders, interchangeably. Since these rights are endowed, or given from God, each of these phrases is adequate. Simply put, *natural law* equals reason, because of its origin (in God), it cannot be given, altered or taken by mankind. It is the very nature of *natural law* that makes it unalienable. Because it is right, it cannot morally be denied.

Each of us is born with the ability to reason and reason correctly. In other words, we all have that little voice in our head and our conscience which tells us what is right and what is wrong. Though false teachings and time can dull or nullify that reasoning. Most of us are born with equal ability to understand and feel natural law in its purity and simplicity. No one would think it morally okay to walk up to a woman on the street and, unprovoked, take her life. We each understand that locking a child in a closet with little food and water is unethical as well as immoral. You would not commandeer or demand half of your neighbor's farm for yourself without compensation. Common sense you say? Common sense is correct. We simply understand those things to be wrong. Many will try to justify them (using religion, retribution, etc.) as being okay, but natural law would tell us otherwise.

The unalienable rights of men cannot be surrendered, taken or transferred to, or from another with or without their consent. These rights are inherent in all men. Obvious in their design and undeniable in nature, these rights can easily be observed while watching a small child just after birth. As infants begin to discover the world around them, eternal and lasting truths are made apparent to them rather quickly. Their young and fragile bodies are at the mercy of those around them for their protection and care. However, the child because of inherent characteristics, will not leave its survival to chance. Since the child has not yet discovered the power, nor developed the ability of speech, he or she is left to communicate in the only way known to them. The very cries of a child are a declaration of principle. In the expressions of pain, hunger, or fatigue, the child proclaims the right to life, to liberty, and to their own individual pursuit of happiness. At such a young age, the child will never be able to articulate it in this manner; it is the substance and meaning behind their expression.

The natural progression of one right upon another is so simplistic in nature, so plain in its reality that as illustrated, a child can know them at birth. Countless numbers of individuals however, have bought into the inauthentic lie that there is no such thing as, that which was penned by the Founders as, *Unalienable*. These great men of our nation's history did not create or bring into being, these rights. They merely worked to elucidate them in such a manner that any man, with any amount of sensible reason about him, could assert with the utmost assurance that these rights are indeed his. Unalienable and unalterable as given by God.

TO MAKE, ALTER, OR ABOLISH

"These no more deserve to be called laws than the rules of a band of robbers might pass in their assembly. For if ignorant and unskill-

ful men have prescribed deadly poisons instead of healing drugs,
these cannot possibly be called physicians' prescriptions; neither
in a nation can a statute of any sort be called a law, even though
the nation, in spite of being a ruinous regulation has accepted
it." —*Cicero*

Because they are given by the *Hand of Divine Providence*, these rights cannot be made, altered, or abolished by government or mankind. An individual who seeks to abstain themselves from these rights does so, only to the degree that they violate the very laws designed to protect the aforementioned rights. Only in the violation can the enjoyment or freedom obtained by virtue of this divinely appointed privilege, be hindered. One individual cannot simply because of his or her own liberty, infringe upon the liberties of another. The rights of all men must be observed for true freedom to exist. Likewise, a government cannot alter or infringe upon the rights of man. As already established, it is man that first creates government and is therefore, its superior. By reason of man's creation of his own government, he can alter the temporal laws by which he is governed. Whether to have three branches of government or four, it does not speak to unalienable rights, but to policy. He still must observe the natural rights of all men.

When individuals begin to legislate away their liberties and freedoms, they keep individuals from defending their rights, and they practice a perversion of the most serious kind. Men who attempt to alter and curtail that which they had not the authority to grant in the first instance, bring great cause for alarm. Unalienable rights, as documented, were granted to men by what the Founders refer to as 'The Laws of Nature and of Nature's God.' Man cannot dispose of, and equally so, cannot confer them upon another as it is impossible to grant to others what was not yours to begin with.

Similar to the understanding of mankind's true position regarding his or her unalienable rights, is the proper structure regarding the government of man. Government in any form or size, is subject to the sovereignty of its people. In the Republican form of government, as was established by our Founders, we see a proverbial line in the sand.

Our *Constitution*, *Declaration of Independence*, and *Bill of Rights* easily illustrates when one's rights are being violated. The exact time and place that government or man steps over the line can be discerned using these documents as a yardstick.

How we as citizens of this great nation choose to be governed is precisely that; our choice. It is through our elected representatives that we either fashion our own shackles or forge our own swords of freedom. Nevertheless, those whom we have elected for our representation have neither the authority, nor the power to make slaves out of free men and women. The rights of one man, as well as the rights of another, are granted by the Creator. Despite the belief that any individual in power, (whether in Congress, a tyrant, or a dictator) has the right to make, alter, or abolish the unalienable rights of man. Truth demands otherwise.

THE DESIGN TO DESTROY
THE RIGHTS OF MEN

> *"One of the most fantastic phenomena of modern times has been the unbelievable success of the Communist conspiracy to enslave mankind. Part of this has been the result of two species of ignorance–ignorance concerning the constitutional requirements needed to perpetuate freedom, and secondly, ignorance concerning the history, philosophy and strategy of World Communism."*
> —Dr. W. Cleon Skousen

If man begins to believe that governments are the source of rights, it follows logically that conspiring men are going to seek the control of government. This would seem an impossible task and the magnitude of the endeavor alone would make most men shrink. However, those with less than desirable designs, who understand the true source of rights, also seek earnestly to understand how a nation could be controlled.

Surely, there will be many individuals who claim that the United States, has beat the monster that is Communism. The Cold War is over, right? To such an individual, I wish to draw attention to what took place during November of 1847. Two men, Karl Marx and Friedrich Engels, were invited to attend the second congress of what was called the *"Federation of the Just"* held in Brussels. While at this congress, Marx and Engels sought to have this congress adopt their views and were commissioned by the congress to write their own declaration of principles. These would later be called *"The Communist Manifesto."* This document would serve as a design and pronouncement to the world of the intentions behind these principles.

The following are the 'Ten Planks' of what became the Communist Manifesto:

- *The abolition of private property and the application of all rents of land to public purposes.*
- *A heavy progressive (or graduated) income tax.*
- *Abolition of all rights of inheritance.*
- *Confiscation of the property of all emigrants and rebels.*
- *Centralization of credit in the hands of the State, by means of a national bank with State capital and an exclusive monopoly.*
- *Centralization of the means of communications and transportation in the hands of the State.*
- *Extension of factories and instruments of production owned by the State. The bringing into cultivation of wastelands, and the improvement of the soil generally in accordance with a common plan.*
- *Equal liability of all to labor. Establishment of industrial armies, especially for agriculture.*
- *Combination of agriculture with manufacturing industries. Gradual abolition of the distinction between town and country, by a more equitable distribution of population over the country.*
- *Free education for all children in public schools. Abolition of children's factory labor in its present form. Combination of education with industrial production.*

Found in number eighteen of the 'Principles of Communism' written by Engles, is a more detailed explanation of their intent. This is where one can distinctly see the design to rob man of these unalienable rights.

"Above all, it will establish a democratic constitution, and through this, the direct or indirect dominance of the proletariat. Direct in England, where the proletarians are already a majority of the people. Indirect in France and Germany, where the majority of the people consists not only of proletarians, but also of small peasants and petty bourgeois who are in the process of falling into the proletariat, who are more and more dependent in all their political interests on the proletariat, and who must, therefore, soon adapt to the demands of the proletariat. Perhaps this will cost a second struggle, but the outcome can only be the victory of the proletariat.

"Democracy would be wholly valueless to the proletariat if it were not immediately used as a means for putting through measures directed against private property and ensuring the livelihood of the proletariat. "It is impossible, of course, to carry out all these measures at once. But one will always bring others in its wake. Once the first radical attack on private property has been launched, the proletariat will find itself forced to go ever further, to concentrate increasingly in the hands of the State all capital, all agriculture, all transport, all trade. All the foregoing measures are directed to this end; and they will become practicable and feasible, capable of producing their centralizing effects to precisely the degree that the proletariat, through its labor, multiplies the country's productive forces.

"Finally, when all capital, all production, all exchange have been brought together in the hands of the nation, private property will disappear of its own accord, money will become superfluous, and production will so expand and man so change that society will be able to slough off whatever of its old economic habits may remain."

–(Frederick Engles, Principles of Communism)

Surely one can see the dangers in the *Socialistic* and *Communistic* philosophies. Sufficient information exists regarding ancient and contemporary civilizations and the utter failure of these destructive ideologies. Only those who seek to remain in power would subject all men to the depravity of control and dispossession of these rights. What moral code is there if a nation, government, and individual wishes only to deprive others of natural, self-evident truths, and unalienable rights? Have we come so far as to say man can enact laws, and governments can enforce regulations to such a degree that the rights of men no longer exist?

Mankind's ability to choose, to decide for oneself the course of action to be taken, is what sets him apart from the beasts of the field. The animal has no power to reason and will act out of instinct. Where mankind will reason, think, and mankind must also take personal accountability. Mankind may willfully seek to absolve himself of personal responsibility, resigning himself to the manipulation of other men, but the hour of reckoning doth eventually come. It is this seeking to avoid responsibility that is the very mask governments will don under the guise of *Social Justice* and *Social Equality* while unable to provide either to any level of success. It is the mask that hides the true face of control, bondage, slavery and desperation it seeks to impose upon its own citizenry.

THE MORALITY OF RIGHTS

"Rights' are a moral concept–the concept that provides logical transition from the principles guiding and individual's actions to the principles guiding his relationship with others–the concept that preserves and protects individual morality in the social context–the link between the moral code of a man and the legal code of a society, between ethics and politics. Individual rights are the means of subordinating society to moral law." —Ayn Rand

Penned in the *Declaration of Independence* are the following words, "That to secure these rights, governments are instituted among men, deriving their just powers from the consent of the governed." Volumes could be recorded upon the study of this singular phrase. The purpose of our government is to secure the rights originally granted by God unto men. Whether or not one chooses to acknowledge the source of the rights they enjoy is up to the individual. The reality of their existence in the lives of all men is indeed real. In securing our rights, it behooves all men to understand and hold government to its proper role. Sovereignty lies with the people, not its government. It is by our consent that we are governed, and by our activism (not complacency and apathy) that we must continue to guard our rights.

In any society of people, a code of values must, first be established for that society to move beyond its initial formation. This code is in part, recognition of self-evident truths. Namely, the members of society exist, therefore the right to their existence is primary. Secondly, their right to decide for themselves how they will live their life and sustain it is theirs, and theirs alone. Finally, the purpose of their life must serve themselves before it can serve the society as a whole. For the whole is made up of individual parts and beyond this recognition, a code of values and laws are set up for the preservation of the rights of each individual within the society. Laws are put in place and penalties are imposed upon those who break these laws. In order for this code of values to be moral and just, its laws and penalties must be designed in such a way that their entire purpose of ensuring the rights of one are not violated by the actions of another. These laws (meant for preservation of rights) and the penalties to be imposed must first be agreed upon by the society as a plurality. Without such an agreement, the society will eventually fail. Those who wish no accountability and no penalty are free to remove themselves from the society and form a new community. Once again, if a new society seeks to deviate from the moral code of which we have outlined, it too will fail.

The preamble to our Constitution reads: "We the People of the United States, in Order to form a more perfect Union, establish Justice, insure domestic Tranquility, provide for the common defense, promote the general Welfare, and secure the Blessings of Liberty to ourselves and our Posterity, do ordain and establish this Constitution for the United States of America." There can be no mistake here where the authority of our government comes from. There is no question the degree and strength our nation has enjoyed by protecting the individual rights of men. The way one chooses to live their life is their individual right (provided they do not violate the rights of another). This is a moral principle, and only a moral people can protect rights as they were granted without seeking to twist, bend, and alter them from their original form. Our government was instituted to make, enact, and administer the laws necessary for the preservation of inherent rights, not for their altercation and abolishment.

CONCLUSION

"With all these blessings, what more is necessary to make us a happy and prosperous people? Still one thing more, fellow citizens—a wise and frugal government, which shall restrain men from injuring one another, which shall leave them otherwise free to regulate their own pursuits of industry and improvement, and shall not take from the mouth of labor the bread it had earned."
—Thomas Jefferson

The rights of life, liberty, and the pursuit of happiness are more than a clever collection of bromides and more than words meant to tickle the ears. These are eternal and unalterable truths. History has shown a great deal of progress for our great nation, in the preservation and exercise of the divine bestowal of rights. To relinquish, trodden under foot, dispose of, or worse, count them as naught, will one day prove to be a most serious transgression. We must fight to preserve that which is rightfully ours, given by our Creator—the Supreme Judge of all mankind. He will truly hold all mankind accountable for our respect and reverence towards such a sacred and noble responsibility as this.

I call upon the famous words uttered by a man dear to all true patriots. They spoke to the people to whom they were directed. Offered up in St. John's Church in Richmond, Virginia on March 23, 1775 by Patrick Henry, "Is life so dear, or peace so sweet, as to be purchased at the price of chains and slavery? Forbid it, Almighty God! I know not what course others may take; but as for me, give me liberty or give me death!" To each, we must ask ourselves where we stand in answer to the very same question.

CHAPTER IV

As its proper role, government is instituted by mankind exclusively to protect unalienable rights.

"That to secure these rights, governments are instituted among men, deriving their just powers from the consent of the governed." —Declaration of Independence

INTRODUCTION

"What has destroyed liberty and the rights of man in every govern-ment which has ever existed under the sun? The generalizing and concentrating all cares and powers into one body..."
—Thomas Jefferson

It is quite easy to slip into a state of ignorance regarding the chronology of the establishment of government. We live in a world which is so *top-down* that believing government to be the *Big Brother* of mankind, appears to be *just the way it is*. It may not feel comfortable to any right-thinking individual, but the government establishment appears nearly omnipotent. The Founders did not see it that way and were downright fearful of such a reality coming to pass.

Thomas Paine recognized the danger of a large, cumbersome governmental system in referring to the imperious, government of

England. In *Common Sense*, he asserted that the country would suffer for many years and not even realize why they were suffering. Likewise, I believe you can get to the point that an organization is so large that finding and rooting out problems is overwhelmingly impossible. Everyone will have a different idea of the problem and each will have a different solution.

The truth about the organization of government is quite the opposite of perceived reality. As previously established in Principle #1, God grants to all men, everywhere, certain, unalienable rights. Because all men desire the rights to be protected, and because they cannot possibly protect them alone, man grants certain protective powers to government. Those functions given to governments, are simple and few. It should be said that they are simple and singular—to protect man's natural rights.

WHAT IS A 'PROPER ROLE?'

"Let the general government be reduced to foreign concerns only… and our general government may be reduced to a very simple organization, & a very unexpensive [sic] one; a few plain duties to be performed by a few servants." —Thomas Jefferson

We define *role* as the part one plays. In a stage show, everyone has an ascribed role, from the lead players to the lighting operators. That part is clearly outlined, learned, and practiced, when it comes time to perform, no one is confused as to what their role is. Silly as it seems, you would not see the lighting operator walk up on stage during the second act, boot the leading female character to the back of the auditorium and finish her solo. If there is a *proper role*, it stands to reason that the antithesis is also true. There must also be an *improper role*.

Though every large organization has properly defined roles within, one should also pull away from the trees long and far enough to see the forest (or proper role) of the organization as a whole. Whether you are a janitor, a sales rep., or a CEO, you have a job description. However, do you know and understand the purpose of the company in general? Do you have a needed and wanted function in the *circle of the life* of the organization? Is the product or service you are providing needed or wanted by the buying public? If so, you and the company you work for has a *proper role*.

This analysis is no different when you look at organizations which are run by tax-payer dollars. Within the government, there are numerous job descriptions. Each one should be analyzed and a determination of whether or not they are necessary should be discussed. As a whole, there are certain things that government has authority to do and many things that they do not. The proper role of a government, thus, should be determined solely by the constitution of the people.

As a people, we will often improperly look to the governmental structure as the first solution to our problems. "There ought to be a law!" is often the rallying cry of the distraught and frustrated masses. However, we would do well to remember that the only role of government, as taught by George Washington, is force. It is nothing more and nothing less. Let me repeat that; the sole purpose of government is to force individuals to do things that they will not otherwise choose to do on their own. I am not advocating that, because government is force, we should have none of it. It should be understood that there is a case to be made for force. There is a place for it in a civilized society. Indeed, force is a useful tool when used with a principled base. However, the test should always come down to the individual. If it is not okay for me to do it to my neighbor, it is never okay to give permission to the government to do it either (Ezra Taft Benson, *The Proper Role of Government*). If that were our litmus test, whether or not force is justified as a consequence of disobedience, we could—and should—wipe out a great majority of the laws currently on our books.

FROM GOD TO MAN TO GOVERNMENT

> *"Society in every state is a blessing, but Government, even in its best state, is but a necessary evil." —Thomas Paine*

We live in a world where the federal (and local) government takes many liberties. A registered letter from Internal Revenue Service arrives in the mail and our heart skips a beat. A highway patrolman pulls us over, requests a search of our vehicle and we readily comply for fear of appearing guilty if we do not. The Senate passes an unmistakably socialistic bill and we do nothing—thus, allowing it to *sail through*. After all, this is the government we are talking about. What can little ol' me possibly do against so formidable a foe?

This was not the America Jefferson, Madison, Franklin, Adams, or Washington envisioned. These men understood the proper line of authority—God to Man, Man to Government.

Just as an employee cannot fire the employer, government has no authority to strip the rights of man. Government is the subordinate of the employer—the people. They work for us. We the people decide their job descriptions, their authorities, their tenure, and, yes, even their salaries.

In order to properly understand where government came from, it is necessary to strip away all of the crushing baggage associated with it. Forget, for a moment, the three branches: 1) the military, 2) the tax system, and 3) the numerous *commissars* who make up the slough we call bureaucracies. Ask the question rather, why was the government created in the beginning?

Let us imagine that a few people were brought together in some deserted land—separated from the rest of the world. Man's nature would dictate that they would soon be drawn to develop a societal relationship with one another. There is benefit in collusion including; unity of strength, a natural inclination to associate, assistance with basic tasks, a combination of materials, knowledge and talents, family structures, and perpetuation of the community. If the community remained cordial to one another, there would be little or no need for governmental structure. History shows, however, that this kind of bliss is not long-lasting. Instead—short of a heavenly society—humanity tends to, relax in its relationships and disagreements surface. This, combined with a desire to protect the society from outside invasion, would naturally spark a need for some type of protective service. In other words, government is created by the society, and is only given authority granted it from those who created it (analogy adapted from Thomas Paine, *Common Sense*).

It cannot be stressed enough that man created government (and not the other way around). Though government may be considered by some to be an *evil*, it should be recognized that it is also quite *necessary*. Proper chronology, however, must be understood that one might remember their own position. If the chicken came before the egg, then the people are the chicken and the government is the egg. Thus, the egg is never superior to the chicken who laid it.

GOVERNMENT'S ONLY ROLE
IS TO PROTECT MAN'S RIGHTS

> "The important thing to keep in mind is that the people who have created their government can give to that government only such powers as they, themselves, have in the first place. Obviously, they cannot give that which they do not possess."
> —Ezra Taft Benson

Taking from the adaptation of Paine's earlier analogy, if there were only two people (you and me) in this make-believe, secluded part of the world, there would be no need for government. In the simplest way, I would be justified in protecting my natural rights and you would be granted the same. Indeed, the only purpose for any organized group is to accomplish together what cannot be accomplished on one's own. Thus, government is instituted to on a full-time basis, protect the natural (God given) rights of the individual. If the Navy is watching our waters, the Marines our shore, the Air Force our skies, the Army our land, and the local Sheriff our personal properties, we are then free to work, travel, and generally go about our lives in peace and security.

The Framers understood this principle completely. The federal power, as defined by the *Constitution*, is very limited. A reading of the document reveals that the powers enumerated to the federal government are few and defined. They include mostly roles relating to foreign interests. The rights granted to the states and acknowledged of the people in contrast, are numerous and amorphous.

Remember, it was the *Bill of Rights* that was the lynchpin in finally allowing the *Constitution* to be ratified by the few, stubborn states which were holding out. They feared the encroachment of the federal structure on the people individually and upon their respective states. In fact, it was because this fear was so inherently accepted that the great debate between the Federalist and Anti-federalists regarding a *Bill of Rights* was waged in the first place. In this great contest, it was not so much a question as to which rights to include in the document as much as it was a question as to whether or not they were even needed at all. When one engages in a direct comparison between the *Federalist Papers* and the *Anti-Federalist Papers*, this idea is palpable.

> "I...affirm that bills of rights, in the sense and to the extent in which they are contended for, are not only unnecessary in the proposed Constitution, but would even be dangerous. They would contain various exceptions to powers not granted; and, on this very account, would afford a colorable pretext to claim more than were granted.
> —Alexander Hamilton, Federalist Papers
>
> No privilege, reserved by the bills of rights, or secured by the State governments, can limit the power granted by this, or restrain any laws made in pursuance of it."
> —Robert Yates, Anti-federalist Papers

Both sides had equally valid points. History has borne out the wisdom in providing a *Bill of Rights*, though encroachments have been made over the years on most of the original ten amendments, and outright denial of any one that has yet to be a reality. Despite a *Bill of Rights* being adopted and implemented as part of the "supreme law of the land," none of them grant more power to the Federal Government than it was originally intended to have. Indeed, the opposite is true. The *Bill of Rights* are intended to secure the rights of men against a tyrannical government taking on more power and authority than it has been granted by the people. Unfortunately, many United States citizens today do not understand this important distinction.

Try this experiment: Find an opportunity to ask a question to your co-workers, family, neighbors, or friends about what they believe the purpose of the Constitution is. It is likely they will respond something like this, "The Constitution is what gives the government its power." It is this answer that you may know they have either not read it or do not understand it.

The Constitution and the *Bill of Rights* are what LIMITS the federal government's power. The control, therefore, is in the people. If the Constitution were understood and strictly interpreted, no fear would ever be justified that the Federal Government might turn to tyranny and usurp the power and rights of the people. It is not in their power to do so.

"But, the Constitution is old and outdated," one might cry. "Surely those men who wrote it could not foresee a time of assault weapons, terrorism, and major economic uncertainty." The argument might be worth entertaining if it were not for two things. First, though Madison might have penned most of it, the rights enshrined therein were not his invention. All principles will stand the test of time and condition. Indeed, one of the defining characteristics of a principle is that it can be followed, with the same result, no matter what the circumstance. The Divine Power that gave us our rights did understand and know of a time when these present-day realities would exist. Second, the Constitution was never intended to become a *living document* in the sense that it could be changed at will by the interpretation of the whims of the contemporary day. No, it was to be interpreted exactly as it was written. Principles are truth and principles govern. They do not change with years. Times are different than they were in 1787, but this is due more to our ignoring and forgetting principles than for any other reason.

The Founders made it very difficult to amend the document. This was not by happenstance. Beware of any movement to amend or change the Constitution of the United States in any way. There are times when it is needed (thus, the provision found in Article V for doing so).

Talk and discussions occur concerning the *enumerated* power of Congress. What can they do? What are they prohibited from doing? Though the average citizen (or congressman for that matter) could not tell you what the enumerated powers are, they are sure whatever laws are currently on the books or being considered, meet the criteria. The fact is, the powers specifically granted to the Legislative body are few in number (depending upon your reading, they number about 20). They range from foreign relations to national defense, from taxation to money. Most are written in plain language that would be difficult to misinterpret. A few (referred to as the *Elastic*, *Welfare*, or *Commerce* clauses) give wiggle room. If taken in their original meaning they are clear as well. Anything else, beyond these 20, is a violation of the permissions granted from the people to their Representatives.

THE CONSTITUTION SHOULD BE A WRITTEN ONE

"A sovereign nation should be governed by a written constitution which carefully delineates the separation of powers and defines the checks and balances assigned to each." —Dr. W. Cleon Skousen

Laws ought to be written in such a way that any literate citizen might easily understand them. As soon as the law grows beyond what the common man can possibly read and reasonably understand, the otherwise law-abiding citizen becomes frustrated, confused, and unable to obey the law. It is not that he is unwilling to do so, but that he is unable to do so. Vague laws make for vague interpretations. One might ask, "Is that lawful?" When the answer is, "Well, that depends on the judge's interpretation of the law" we know we have gone too far.

It was for this very purpose that the Constitution of the United States was drafted. The Founder's knew that though based on Natural Law, it was necessary and prudent to put these rights of every man into a written and concise document that would stand the test of the ages. Surely, of all governmental documents, the Constitution is one of the most succinct (the entire draft fits on four 23 5/8" x 28 ¾" hand-written pages). Though written at a time where the language of the day is difficult for a 21st Century dweller to interpret (try reading the *Federalist Papers*), it is understandable to even a high school student.

IF IT GOES BEYOND LIFE, LIBERTY, AND PROPERTY, IT HAS GONE TOO FAR

"I realize that when I give my consent to the adoption of a law, I specifically instruct the police – the government – to take either the life, liberty, or property of anyone who disobeys that law. Furthermore, I tell them that if anyone resists the enforcement of the law, they are to use any means necessary – yes, even putting the lawbreaker to death or putting him in jail – to overcome such resistance. These are extreme measures but unless laws are enforced, anarchy results." —Ezra Taft Benson

By definition, the government as an entity, cannot produce anything of monetary value. It merely creates a sense of security. No government anywhere, at any time, has ever produced a single dime. The creation of a paper currency, whether backed by gold or not, does not constitute value production. Accomplishments are evidence of work performed and ideas implemented. A government cannot work or implement without those who have been elected to perform the necessary functions. This sentiment may be difficult to grasp because we live in a society which often touts the *accomplishments* of government in the same fashion that the business world is heralded. Headlines scream, "New Government Program Will Create 5,000 New Jobs," or "Government Revenue Increases with Proposed Bill." When you separate the hyperbole from reality, it becomes clear what is actually transpiring. Though a particular government entity can be *solvent*, like as the Federal Housing Administration (FHA) has historically been, it requires tax dollars to get started and tax dollars to make up the difference if they have a bad year. You must trace the money to its source in order to find the answer. Furthermore, *the government* is simply a broad (and misleading) term for *the people*. The *Declaration of Independence* says it best when it remind us that governments "…[derive] their just powers from the consent of the governed." If any particular governmental bureaucracy is *successful*, it is *the people* who make it so."

It is easy to slip into the mind-set that government is a money tree, an endless source of revenue from whence any problem can be solved. "Where shall we get the money for that program?" one might ask. The answer? *The government*. Ask a bureaucrat where he gets his paycheck. His answer? *The government*. The answer is always *the government* as if the concept is some magical, mystical pot of gold just sitting there for the taking. We tend to forget, however, what that government really is. A system of taking from one to give to another. If instead, we would use the term *the people*, (a proper, and more fitting description of reality), it is likely that less governmental programs would exist and fewer bureaucrats would have jobs. Imagine the following: Where shall we get the money for that program? The answer? We will take it from the people. Ask a bureaucrat in such a transparent world where he gets his paycheck. The answer? I will obtain it forcibly from the people. The honesty in such an answer insists on accountability.

The bottom line is this, improper government in its most simple form, is plunder (theft) by force (law). Legal plunder indeed, but still plunder nonetheless. Remember, legality does not equal morality. When a business needs additional capital, it must produce it. When the government needs more money, it simply takes it.

> *"But how is the legal plunder to be identified? Quite simply. See if the law takes from some persons what belongs to them, and gives it to other persons to whom it does not belong. See if the law benefits one citizen at the expense of another by doing what the citizen himself cannot do without committing a crime...legal plunder can be committed in an infinite number of ways. Thus we have an infinite number of plans for organizing it: tariffs, protection, benefits, subsidies, encouragements, progressive taxation, public schools, guaranteed jobs, guaranteed profits, minimum wages, a right to relief, a right to the tools of labor,*

free credit, and so on, and so on." – (Frederic Bastiat, The Law).

Though a certain governmental program may appear on the surface to be well-meaning, appropriate, and even *Christian* in its nature one must always remember that *force* is used to obtain the money to administer any program. Granted, it is not usually seen in this light because the masses will simply comply and give up their money (in the form of taxes) for the program. But, what if one refuses? If you follow any law to its natural conclusion, at the end of the road one finds a gun.

Bureaucrats are created to enforce (or force) laws upon those who would not otherwise choose to comply on their own. Are you willing to see welfare programs ultimately enforced at the point of a gun? As with every law, there is a punishment affixed. Refusing to give your money to a federal welfare program is called 'tax evasion' and is typically punished by a fine for the first offense. What if you refuse to pay the fine? Likely, a larger fine would then be imposed. If you refused that fine, a levy on your assets could ensue. Should you refuse to give them up, it can be reasonably assumed that a warrant for your arrest may be the next logical step. What if you feel this law is unjust and dig your heels in? In reality, the government (the enforcer of the law) could come to your house and force your detention. Ultimately if you continue to resist, their only way of taking you to jail would be at the point of a gun. Every law, every dictate, and every *charitable* welfare program implemented by the government, is eventually enforced in the end with gun.

If the above referenced quote from Benson is true, therein lays the great tenet in which any law ought to be judged, "Am I willing to see a gun employed in the enforcement of this law?" If the answer is no, the law should be removed.

The next time a new plan is proposed for some goodly cause, ask yourself this, "Would I be willing to put a gun in the face of my neighbor in order to obtain the revenue necessary?" If the answer is *no*, it is not your right to give your elected officials permission to do the dirty work for you. The Founders understood this, and if one studies Article I, Section 9 of the Constitution, no authority for the Federal Government to provide for the welfare of the citizens will be found.

What about the poor? What about the needy? What about those who just cannot provide for themselves? Shouldn't the government's role be to help such a people? First of all, it is obvious to any observant person that such people do exist. Even well-meaning, hard-working Americans can fall on hard times. Are programs needed for such circumstances? The answer to this question is yes, but from whom? Why should a free people be forced to administer it (through the federal government) when they would likely do it on their own anyway? It is in our God-given nature to do so.

Instead, let the people exercise their Christian virtues without compulsion. Every effort should be made to assist the individual in assisting themselves. Agency implies stewardship and seeking to take that stewardship from another will often lead to dependency and misery. If the individual is indeed in a hopeless situation, the next best support structure should be the family (immediate and extended). Then comes the church, the neighborhood, and lastly the LOCAL government. The more local the help, the more able the helpers are to understand the situation, recognize the needs, and detect any deception. Would you trust a long-distance doctor, one whom had no knowledge of your personal health, to diagnose your condition over a phone or through a letter, and prescribe a medical treatment for you? Why then would we trust the Federal Government to determine and distribute welfare? At a federal level, it is impossible for those making the decisions to know and intimately understand the individual circumstances of those accepting the welfare. Consequently, deception and fraud exists on a large scale. At a local level, charity is far more difficult to abuse.

We would be wise to consider the natural consequences of such action. God is the author of nature, and He has imposed certain consequences that are bound to follow any given action. When we, our family, our churches, our community, our government seek to relieve or cover the natural consequences of action or inaction, the consequences can come in different—often heavier—consequences.

Jefferson was quite outspoken on the subject of providing for others—but individually, rather than through governmental programs. He believed that it was everyone's duty (himself included) to pay a percentage of income to charitable purposes, (*Thomas Jefferson to Rogers and Slaughter*, L&B.11.92-93). He also understood the truth that when we offer such charities out of love rather than governmental force, the Natural Law would bless us with happiness (*Thomas Jefferson to Thomas Law*, L&B.14.141).

As Americans, we have historically followed this advice. We have relied upon the charity of individuals to solve the nation's welfare problems. Consequently, we have traditionally been the shining beacon on a hill to the rest of the nations in the few numbers of cases per capita (Ezra Taft Benson, *The Proper Role of Government*).

One of the biggest problems with a social welfare program is that it steals from the people…twice. It first, takes in the form of plundering their goods—their money. When one is forced to pay exorbitant taxes for special programs, it is self-evident that there is less gold in his purse for him to be able to give willingly. Secondly, it embezzles in the form of stripping their charitable attitude. There is a natural inclination to justify the lack of giving to the poor by feeling that one *already gave on April 15th in great abundance.* Rather than seeing a need and being able to provide relief, we like Scrooge, cry, "Are there no prisons?" (Charles Dickenson, *A Christmas Carol*). Are there no poor houses? Are there no State-run programs? I give my fair share. Why should I need to give more?

When the government establishes a program to help this class of people they take more than money from the citizenship to administer the program. They are raping virtue from the charitable heart of an otherwise understanding and giving profiteer.

There once was a group of neighbors who learned about a local, free lunch program. The program was being offered through a grant from federal sources. The name of the program was "The Child Nutrition Act." Sounds like a great program. Who is not for helping children get better nutrition?

The program was administered at the local elementary school. Each day, during the summer, food was cooked and served to anyone under the age of 18. Though it was touted as a program for the poor and needy, no verification of income level or need was ever completed. Anyone, at any time could come to the school, fill up their plate, and enjoy a meal. Oh, and it was free!

Based on the homes they lived in, the cars they drove, and the clothes they wore, it was obvious that many of those attending the daily lunch were not part of the poor and needy the program was intended for. When asked, the response was, "We just do not want to make lunch for our kids every day. It is easier to load them in the SUV and drive two blocks to the school. We figure we have to pay for it anyway. We might as well take advantage of it."

Let's explore that logic for just a moment. The former self-justification for their actions is just pure laziness. Laziness is a violation of true principles and carries with it its own consequences. The 'we pay for it anyway' excuse is more logical, but still full of holes. It is natural, when compelled to give, to desire at least something in return. In their minds, they sent in their check on April 15th, just like everyone else. They have as much right to be enjoying the free lunch as anyone else. After all, they already paid for it, right?

The problem with this kind of thinking is two-fold. First, if the program violates true principles (which this one clearly does), it is a violation of personal principle to participate. Actions have consequences. Second, the participation in such a program only encourages the very growth of the program. The local food services supervisor was interviewed by the newspaper. She was quoted as saying, "Every year we increase new families. But we don't seem to lose established families." Another district supervisor cried, "It's a shame (more people don't apply) because the program is here for that purpose" (The Post Register, July 2, 2009, pg A1 and A4). In their minds, more and more needy families are eating where they would otherwise starve—clearly not the *reality. But you can, rest-assured, that if the local supervisors see the increased attendance in that light, the lawmakers will see it that way as well. Thus, resulting in support for this program and continued need for more programs like it. The old axiom, there is no such thing as a free lunch is apropos.*

CONCLUSION

"Whenever we attempt to mend the scheme of Providence and to interfere in the Government of the World, we had need be very circumspect lest we do more harm than Good."
—Benjamin Franklin

Unalienable rights have, and will, always exist. They are granted unto men by a benevolent and loving Heavenly Father. Despite what individuals, religions, organizations, or governments may do to deny these rights, they will continue to exist in the hearts of all men. Each of us is born into this world with innate knowledge of these rights. When they are taken or oppressed, the human soul cries out for their restoration.

In order to help protect and preserve such rights, men socialize and form government. It is the purpose and sole-function of such governments to protect and maintain these God-given rights. No matter how noble, honorable, charitable, or good a governmental practice or program is, if it goes beyond the protection of rights, it has gone beyond that authority it naturally has. Whenever a government strips mankind of what it has no right to give, alter, or take, you may know that such government has forgotten who she is and has slipped into repression.

CHAPTER V

─── ❧ ───

It is the right of the people to alter or abolish an abusive government.

"The tree of liberty must be refreshed from time to time with the blood of patriots and tyrants." — *Thomas Jefferson*

INTRODUCTION

"Political power automatically gravitates toward the center, and the purpose of the Constitution is to prevent that from happening. The centralization of political power always destroys liberty by removing the decision-making function from the people on the local level and transferring it to the officers of the central government." — *Dr. W. Cleon Skousen*

A rose bush has got to be one of the most beautiful landscaping plants in a yard. They are typically large and full of blooming flowers. Taking care of a rose bush, however, can be an interesting ordeal. In addition to the needed soil, sun, and water, trimming and pruning should occur frequently. Those who understand how a rose bush grows know that each year, many new canes (stems) grow; leaving old, decaying canes behind. If left unattended, those older canes takes the entire plant to disease, and break or die all together. Most of the time, the pruning can take place in a systematic, and routine process. Cut a little here and cut a little there. Frequently, it is customary that a more drastic, *cutting down* of the rose bush be carried out. This is not another mild trimming. A seemingly harsh task, the plant must be cut off with no more than 18 inches showing above the ground. If it is not, it may grow wild, untamed, and unattractive. When observing the bare stump, this may seem a cruel act, if done regularly, it will keep the plant in check and continue to allow it to grow into a stunning flowering bush.

There is an analogy between the rose bush and the metaphoric tree of liberty. Due to the nature of government, if left to grow un- checked, it can (and historically always has) become a monstrosity that is cumbersome and difficult to tame. Most of the time, this main- tenance can be taken care of by *trimming* government on a regular basis. This is best accomplished through the constant and regular turn-over of personnel.

When government has grown to the point of centralization in re- sistance to personal liberties, it has gone beyond the rights intended and bestowed by man. Since government has no rights, except what it is granted by men, it becomes the duty of man—the creator of government—to re-capture its invention.

In Mary Shelley's Frankenstein, the doctor creates a monster much larger and stronger than a typical man. Though never intending it to be so, Doctor Frankenstein's monster becomes too large and too unruly to control. Several people are consequently killed, including the doctor's wife, father, and brother. The creation has, in a sense, destroyed the creator's life. Is the same not true with the monster of government? Though we created it, it often seems larger than our ability to control.

THE FRAMERS AND INDIVIDUAL RIGHTS

"Notwithstanding the different modes in which [the federal and state governments] are appointed, we must consider both of them as substantially dependent on the great body of the citizens of the United States…The ultimate authority, wherever the derivative

*may be found, resides in the people alone....Truth, no less than
decency, requires that the event in every case should be supposed
to depend on the sentiments and sanction of their common constituents." —James Madison*

It has become taboo to even broach the subject of making a
major change in government. The status quo has somehow become
a *holy grail* to lovers of liberty. To speak of revolution puts you in the
same category with the blasphemers of religion. Is it treason to have
a debate about the current state of our affairs, the path we continue
to travel, or how and when to make a U-turn?

The concepts talked about in this chapter must be understood in
the context of the Framer's mindset. The Fathers of our country were
mindful of the nature of man and his relationship to government. As
discussed earlier, government is an outgrowth of man's inability to
protect his individual rights alone. Government is created by man,
thus can be changed or dissolved by man.

If one takes the view that man is superior to government, the concepts of altering or even dissolving and then rebuilding a government
which has become abusive, is better accepted. In the end, it is 'We the
People' who are in charge. We are the horse. Government is the cart.

ALTERING GOVERNMENT

*"We, the people are the rightful masters of both Congress and the
courts, not to overthrow the Constitution, but to overthrow men
who pervert the Constitution." —Abraham Lincoln*

Often, it feels that we the people have been made to feel as though
we are second class citizens. Instead of people directing the mind
and actions of the elected, we find the *servants of the people* steam-
rolling legislation and listening to party leaders or lobbyists over and
above their own constituents. We must not forget that we sign their
paycheck. We decide who gets elected and who goes home.

It was determined early on that the best form of Republican Government was one that had potentially a high turnover. In business, turnover is destructive. In government, it is quite the opposite. The idea of career politicians was repugnant to the Founders. In fact, it is telling to observe that to the country's Fathers, the more powerful the office, the less amount of time ought to be its occupants. Conversely, the less power an office holder had, the more time could safely be spent there. In other words, the more liberty granted to a particular office, the quicker ought to be the election of the occupant. That way, the power bestowed upon such must be constantly controlled by reliance upon the voters (James Madison, *Federalist Papers* #52).

Most of the Founders envisioned an electorate who came from the common people and quickly returned from whence they came. They should make laws based on an understanding, that they would live under the same laws they were passing. Because they were *one of them*, more restraint from tyranny and a desire to please their constituents would be had. It was this principle that perpetuated the short two-year terms of the House of Representatives. This was the body *of the people* and the body which had primary control of the purse strings. They would need to return often to the electorate for *permission* to continue to serve.

Even with an aversion to long, political tenures, the Framers of the *Constitution* saw the wisdom in avoiding prescribed term limits. To them, limited terms were a prerogative of the electorate alone. If the public trust was maintained, re-election was an option. By being dependent upon the voters for their trust, politicians would have an increased incentive to represent the people.

Furthermore, politicians themselves had the decency in the beginning, to adhere to the greater good of limiting their own stays in office. In fact, it was not until 1947 that term limits for the President and Vice President were added to the *Constitution* (Amendment 24). George Washington set the precedence when he would have easily won a third term in office and declined. Subsequently, no President served more than two terms in office until Franklin Roosevelt, who was elected to five terms, but passed away before his last term ended.

It is through the frequent elections of our representatives that an abusive government is most easily altered. In order to be effective, the people must be educated on current events, organized, willing to be active, not just on Election Day.

The alternative to a change in guards, is a change in the laws the guards perpetuate. Laws are the fruit of the servants. In the United States, there are hundreds of thousands of laws, despite the fact that the Founding Fathers never intended it to be that way. Instead, laws were to be both limited and checked. It is impossible to follow the laws if they are too numerous or too confusing to even understand.

In order to guard against the oppressive mountain of laws we have today and in order to not pass them on to our children, Thomas Jefferson taught, that a law ought to "naturally [expire] at the end of 19 years. If it be enforced longer, it is an act of coercion, and not of right. It may be said that the succeeding generation exercising in fact the power of repeal, this leaves them as free as if the *Constitution* or law has been expressly limited to 19 years only" (*Letters of Thomas Jefferson, Letter to James Madison*, September 6, 1789). That kind of utopian sunset statute is not currently in force. However, just as our politicians must abide by voter-enforced term-limits, so can laws be periodically changed or deleted from existence.

All laws can be broken down into two categories. In Latin, the terms are *Male in Se* and *Mala Prohibita*. The former, describes laws against things that are inherently wrong. These include laws against murder, rape, theft, fraud, violence, etc. The later, are laws that are against things which are only wrong because someone, somewhere decided they should be wrong. Examples in this section include speed limits, littering, seatbelt laws, loitering, gun control, and talking on a cell phone while driving.

The main reason the later laws get passed is because to the people voting for them they make sense. Who has not been offended by the amount of trash scattered on our highways? Who hasn't, been irritated by a group of skateboarders loitering around the outside of a public building? Ever been on a peaceful, winter walk with your spouse and had to go around a sidewalk because the owner did not care to remove the snow? *There ought to be a law*, right?

Just because something is annoying, immoral, or unethical does not make another law requisite. Whatever happened to dealing with the problem ourself? No, I am not advocating vigilante justice. I am simply saying, that if you, and enough of your neighbors cordially approached the owner of the unshoveled sidewalk with your complaints, do you not believe that in most cases, the problem would be solved?

Altering government begins with thinking. Often these laws get on the books and stay on the books, not because they are good laws, but because citizens are either ignorant or apathetic, or both. Are you tired of big government running your life? Then, do something about it! Start by holding your elected officials accountable.

The Founder's were strong believers in a Representative Republican form of government. They wanted the people to have a say, but not a strict majority rule. That is the system we currently have. That is the system that can be, and should be, utilized. In other words, our first line of defense against an ever-growing government usurpation of rights, is to work within the system to change the system.

ABOLISHING GOVERNMENT

> *"I hold it that a little rebellion now and then is a good thing…*
> *It is a medicine necessary for the sound health of government."*
> *–Thomas Jefferson*

Just as every gas station has a large, red shutoff switch IN CASE OF EMERGENCY, the Framer's provided a similar device for government. IN CASE OF EMERGENCY, or in other words, *in case this government does what so many in history have also done*, push this button. The button provided is the right of the people to completely abolish an abusive government.

There may come a time when the written laws are in violation of the laws of nature. In this instance, and when those laws become oppressive to the point that progression and liberty is stifled, natural law may trump.

Before a people take that step, it would be well to remember that the abolishing of a government is not an end, but a beginning. Routing out a cancer is not a permanent fix, one must also replace the void with something better. Being a student of history and understanding the consequences of anarchy, Thomas Jefferson was quite anxious during the Revolutionary War that the no one was actively formulating a structure for the new government once the war was won (Dr. W. Cleon Skousen, *The Majesty of God's Law*, 415).

Though the right of the people to remove a tyrannical government is clearly established, the purpose for such must also be carefully analyzed. An *entrance strategy* (of the new government), should be contemplated before the *exit strategy* (of the abusive government), should be considered. In other words, no government at all can ever be considered a sustainable solution. Anarchy, in opposition to an authoritarian government, can be as bad, if not worse, than the original. Exchanging a soiled diaper for no diaper at all will not provide a long term solution to the problem at hand. The ability to rebuild with the majority in agreement, is desirable if abolishment of a government is considered necessary.

WHAT CONSTITUTES AN "ABUSIVE GOVERNMENT?"

"Great mistakes in the ruling part. Many wrong and inconvenient laws and all the slips of human frailty will be borne by the people without mutiny or murmur, but if a long train of abuses, prevarications and artifices, all tending the same way, make the design visible to the people, and they cannot but feel what they lie under, and see whither they are going, it is not to be wondered at that they should then rouse themselves, and endeavor to put the rule into such hands which may secure to them the ends for which government was at first erected." —John Locke

Once a clear understanding of the rights of the people to alter their government is understood, the next question is When? At what point is a government considered too big, too unruly, too oppressive, or too tyrannical to be tolerated? The answer to that important question is not completely cut and dry, but certainly have signs to look for.

First of all, the abuses must be many and long. Historians will typically describe the precursor to the Boston Tea Party as a frustrating time over *Taxation without Representation*. Though technically correct, this simplistic view of historical facts leave much unsaid. If taxes on tea were the only issue facing the Sons of Liberty, our current state of government, would indeed signal a need for a bloody revolution. On the contrary, when the Sons of Liberty boarded the ships in Boston Harbor, it was only after a very long list of abuses from the Crown had led to justify such an action. These abuses included infringements on freedom of expression and the press, quartering of troops in private homes, unwarranted searches of private property, etc.

There is a reason the *Bill of Rights* were written as they were. Though meant to be followed perpetually, they were not prophetic. In nature rather, most of these rights had already been denied the authors of the Bill in the past. Furthermore, the tea was not dumped in the harbor on the day it arrived. Samuel Adams and his cohorts waited a full 19 days after the ships had arrived, all the while, pleading for the Royal Governor to do the right thing. The Governor would not. The *Tea Party*, (precursor to the American Revolution) was a last resort.

If one takes a careful reading of the *Declaration of Independence*, it becomes obvious that, before independence from England was declared, the list of oppressions were numerous and had occurred for many years. It was not just one or two issues which screamed, "Revolution!" Jefferson penned it thus, "When a long train of abuses and usurpations, pursuing invariably the same object evinces a design to reduce them under absolute despotism, it is their right, it is their duty, to throw off such government, and to provide new guards for their future security" (*Declaration of Independence*). The key phrase here is "long train of abuses." The answer to this question, "How long?"

AN ADDITIONAL WORD ABOUT REVOLUTION

"This country, with its institutions, belongs to the people who

inhabit it. Whenever they shall grow weary of the existing Government, they can exercise their 'constitutional' right of amending it or their 'revolutionary' right to dismember or overthrow it."
-Abraham Lincoln

The question still yet to be settled then is when that revolutionary right, can or should be invoked and at what point are the people justified in a bloody revolution?

Under English political theory, it was illegal to demand restitution from government, over abuse or individual wrongs. It had to be the consent of the majority before revolute was warranted (Paline Maier, *From Resistance to Revolution*).

Indeed, the law of redress from an abusive government has long been recognized as a natural law of the people. Some great philosophers of government (including John Locke) add the *majority* factor. He, as well as others, believed that before revolution could be justified, the *majority* of citizens should feel the oppression and tyrannical hand resting upon their liberties. Dr. Skousen also taught that there must be a majority of the people in favor of revolution before it be justified (*The 5,000 Year Leap*).

This philosophy, if true, flies in the face of those rebels of 1775. For if Historians, David McCullough, Paul H. Smith, and Robert Calhoon's estimates are correct, a small majority of individuals supported revolution, but it was far less than that (David McCullough, *A Man Worth Knowing*, Imprimis, May 2006; Paul H. Smith, *"The American Loyalists: Notes on Their Organization and Numerical Strength,"* William and Mary Quarterly 3d Series, Vol. 25 (Apr. 1968), 262, 262n7, 267-269; and Robert M. Calhoon, *A companion to the American Revolution*, (2000). Yet, most Americans would doubt the Colonist's right to rebel as they did, and when they did.

"If these illegal acts have extended to the majority of the people, or if the mischief and oppression has light only on some few, but in such cases as the precedent and consequences seem to threaten all, and they are persuaded in their consciences that their laws, and with them, their estates, liberties, and lives are in danger, and perhaps their religion too, how they will be hindered from resisting illegal force used against them I cannot tell. This is an inconvenience, I confess, that attends all governments whatsoever" (John Locke, *The Second Treaties on Government*). It is interesting to note in Locke's statement that he did not say "the majority should rise up together." Rather, his justification for rebellion is on the numbers of people the ABUSE'S touch, or even MIGHT touch upon. In a preceding paragraph, Locke appears to clarify his statement by referring to the ABILITY of the minority to defend itself against a tyrannical government, rather than the RIGHT to do so. "For if it reach no farther than some private men's cases, *though they have a right* to defend themselves, and to recover by force what by unlawful force is taken from them, yet the right to do so will not easily engage them in a contest wherein they are sure to perish; *it being as impossible for one or a few oppressed men to disturb the government* where the body of the people do not think themselves concerned in it, as for a raving madman or heady malcontent to overturn a well-settled state, the people being as little apt to follow the one as the other" (ibid. 208, emphasis added). He is saying that even a few would have the right to defend themselves from oppression, but may not have the power to succeed. Volumes could be written about Randy Weaver and David Koresh that discusses taking on the federal government alone is not advisable.

In the current context, the word *majority* is also curious. Though most of us would rightly interpret the word as describing a figure of over 50% of a given population, there is some argument for another definition. In Webster's 1829 Dictionary, Daniel Webster, a contemporary of the Founding Fathers, gives one explanation of the word *majority* as *the state of being greater*. Two quarters are greater than three dimes, though they represent a minority number of coins. If five friends congregate and three of the five decide to physically abuse a puppy, the two who rise up against the measure represent a more powerful majority. Indeed, when truth and right are on the side of a people (whether he be one or many), he is a majority.

The Children of Israel understood this tenet. After the Lord had reduced their numbers to a mere 300, Gideon battled the copious

Midianite Army and they were still quite successful (*KJV* Judges 7). "They that be with us are more than they that be with them" (*KJV* 2 Kings 6:16). Though in literal numbers, the opposite was true. Rest assured, if and when the time for a revolution comes, there will be no doubt in the minds of those *in tune* when that time has arrived.

CONCLUSION

"I have lived, Sir, a long time and the longer I live the more convincing proof I see of this truth: that God governs the affairs of men. If a sparrow cannot fall without His notice, is it possible that an empire can rise without His aid." -Benjamin Franklin

It is not a stretch to conclude that two facts exist; First, America is currently experiencing many challenges and abuses for which the natural man should not be required to suffer. Second, government can be a formidable foe. As sure as God exists, man has two arrows in his quiver which are his right, and his duty to employ. The first being the right to amend, and the second to abolish an abusive government.

Our prerequisite step should be that of improvement. The system still works, but the system must be used. The Founders gave us the tools to change the government every two years. At the ballot box, the Representatives of each state can be thrown out and those who will live by true principles can be installed.

Altering government is by far, the better choice of the alternative. "Prudence, indeed, will dictate that governments long established should not be changed for light and transient causes; and accordingly all experience hath shown that mankind are more disposed to suffer, while evils are sufferable, than to right themselves by abolishing the forms to which they are accustomed" (*Declaration of Independence*). Revolution should be seen in similar fashion to the way the President of the United States employ the *nuclear football*. The very threat, will in most cases, cause the people to keep their government in check. Using the ultimate weapon, though necessary at times, should not be taken lightly. It has unintended consequences, some of which we do not yet know. It cannot be done with one small organization, and it should not be done at all if avoidance is still an option. One cannot be justified in participating in a revolution unless all other resources have been exhausted first. If all else fails, revolution may be the only solution. The key phrase however, is *if all else fails.*

CHAPTER VI

❧⚶❧

All mankind are justified before God in the defense of unalienable rights.

"From my cold, dead hands." —**Charlton Heston**

INTRODUCTION

"Resistance to tyrants is obedience to God." —*Thomas Jefferson*

Just as mankind has been endowed with certain, unalienable rights, he has also been endowed by the Creator, with the right to defend such. Because rights are given from Him and cannot be taken by society or government, man is justified in doing what is necessary to protect and preserve those rights.

Throughout history laws have been passed and public sentiment has been changed, but the defense of our natural rights cannot be revoked. One can be found in an interesting dichotomy if caught between a police-enforced law and a *natural right*. It is probable that, in the defense of unalienable rights, one will find himself pitted against the very law that is actively trying to take such rights away. At that moment, he finds himself in a moral dilemma between *being a good citizen* and the defending of Natural Law. In other words, he may be sandwiched between what society sees as lawful and what

God defines as naturally right.

RIGHT TO DEFEND LIFE TRUMPS ALL

"Self-defense, as it is justly called the primary law of nature, so it is not, neither can it be in fact, taken away by the law of society."
—William Blackstone

Imagine if you will, that you have been invited to a neighbor's home for dinner. After a lovely meal you are gathered in the host's living room for pleasant conversation. As you are casually discussing the politics of the day, the host stands up, nonchalantly circles around to the back of your chair, suddenly wraps a cord around your neck and begins to choke you. Though this situation would be highly out of place and unexpected, ask yourself how you might react. What would you think? What would you do?

It is unimaginable that anyone in this particular scenario would not do everything in their power to stop what was happening. Likely, you would try to pull the cord or pull their hands until you were free. You would twist and turn, struggle, kick, thrash and do everything you could possibly do to free yourself. I doubt anyone would think to themselves, "Okay, my neighbor is trying to choke me. This really hurts, but I probably should not do anything about it. After all, this is his house and he has the right to do whatever he would like in his own home." Preposterous! Though the host has the right to private property, the right to life—your life—surely trumps. Certainly no law or boundary is off limits when you are fighting to live. The right to survive surmounts all other rights!

Men are born with a desire to preserve their lives. We naturally have an aversion to death and will do almost anything to remain breathing. Society may try to lessen or diminish that deep-rooted conviction, but it still exists. It is vigilantly there, and it will surface whenever the time presents itself.

Furthermore, as a member of society, one is under the moral obligation to protect family, friends, neighbors, and even complete strangers from a threat to their lives. To feel that sense of duty, is human. Each unalienable right is worth defending and each unalienable right impacts others.

RIGHT TO DEFEND LIBERTY

"All might be free if they valued freedom, and defended it as they should." —Samuel Adams.

The terms 'freedom' and 'liberty' are often used interchangeably and rightfully so. For it is liberty which gives man the freedom to act, think, and speak in a manner pleasing to oneself. It is what it means to be an American. It is the quintessential difference between 'us' and 'them.'

Not only are we as members of the human race, born with the natural right of self-defense, we inherited a history of such from our forefathers. Much blood has been spilt on the dirt within our borders and abroad to win our liberties. We must defend that legacy amidst all costs. Our ancestors would be remorseful if we did not.

The defense of liberty is tricky. On the one hand, the Founders set up a system for the very purpose of protecting liberty. On the proverbial other hand, the system only works as long as the system is in place. It was the former US Ambassador to Mexico who, in 1944 reminded us "we stand in danger of losing our liberties, and that once lost, only blood will bring them back" (Joshua Reuben Clark, Undersecretary of State for President Coolidge, *Conference Report,* Apr. 1944).

It therefore behooves us as free men to utilize the ballot box and pulpit while they are still at our disposal. Liberty must be used to defend liberty till liberty is lost. Once it is gone, it takes courage, and often the ultimate cost of laying down of the first right—life—in order to restore it again.

RIGHT TO DEFEND PROPERTY

"It is the protection and safeguarding of property that government was established for in the first place. Indeed, the very end

of government is to preserve that which belongs to its citizens."

— *John Locke*

It is a right that is often taken for granted, because it is so engrained in the day-to-day normality of living in a free society. The right to own, sell, distribute, share, and use property is essential in a free society. Collectively, these freedoms are encapsulated in the right of the happiness pursuit.

A look at defense laws in most states, will reveal that justification for deadly force is often tolerable for not only life and liberty, but also for property. In recent years, *Castle Doctrine* (Defense of Habitation) laws have become quite fashionable and have been passed by state legislatures across the country. These laws place the burden of proof back on the perpetrator of the crime rather than on the defender if deadly force is used to protect one's estate.

When the Founders spoke of property, they didn't just mean it in the form of real estate. As eternally enshrined in the *Bill of Rights*, "The right of the people to be secure in their persons, houses, papers, and effects…shall not be violated…" (Amendment 4). Surely property includes land, homes, effects, amenities, improvements, original ideas, intellectual claims, business concepts, etc. Thus, defending each of these, is or should be justified.

THE RIGHT TO OWN AND BEAR ARMS IS A VITAL PRESERVATION OF LIBERTY

"Though the use of arms should be reserved and used only as a last resort—it is still a resort. "…always [remember] that an armed and trained militia is the firmest bulwark of republics--that without standing armies their liberty can never be in danger, nor with large [armies] safe." —James Madison

When a government is aware of the mass citizen ownership and training of guns, it must remain in check regarding the oppression, diminishing of, or outright restriction of the three pillars of unalienable rights. Just as the mere possession of nuclear weapons tends to keep other nations at bay, the mere ownership of small weapons will keep our leaders on their proverbial toes. Indeed, the rights of the people to keep and bear arms is the ultimate check on government.

The principles justifying the ownership and use of arms by a free people were not original with the Founders. As in all principles, they have always existed and will continue to always be. A seemingly defenseless victim is a more alluring target to a criminal than one seen as able to 'hold her own.' Facts show that in states with conceal carry laws in effect, the idea that a potential victim could be armed is enough of a deterrent to potential criminals that crime statistics are dramatically affected (John Lott, *More Guns, Less Crime*).

Likewise, the Founding Fathers understood intimately how an otherwise good government could quickly become oppressive and tyrannical. Surely, this is why the Revolutionary War was fought in the first place. In fact, many believe the shot heard around the world was over taxes, but true history is that it was instead over gun control. On April 19, 1775, British General Thomas Gage dispatched men to Concord to seize powder, shot and arms from the Colonists. That is where it all began. These patriots knew that if their arms were seized, they were powerless against this formidable governmental foe.

ALL GUN CONTROL IS A VIOLATION OF PRINCIPLE

"When you outlaw guns, then only the outlaws have the guns."
—Unknown

The idea that the American people could ever be disarmed of the rights to gun ownership was repulsive to the Founders as it was in several generations to come. Though they preserved the right in the Second Amendment, it was a foregone conclusion that for government to deny this right would be to trample Natural Law itself. Indeed, the first real prohibition on guns was not a prohibition at all, but a tax. In 1934, just after the Twenty-first Amendment had rendered a governmental institution (Alcohol Tax Unit—later to become the ATF) worthless, a national tax on certain weaponry (and accessories) went into effect. Because it was a tax, and not an outright ban, the people allowed it to happen. Like the frog in the proverbial boiling water, taxes turned in to blatant bans and finally gun bans became commonplace.

Though many politicians will dawn their orange vests, stand in front of the cameras, and tell you about their days in the fields shooting rabbits, the Second Amendment is not now nor ever has ever been about hunting. Instead, it is all about the preservation of our liberties. In virtually all countries where mass murder and genocide has happened, it was preceded by gun control, gun registration, and eventually gun confiscation. All-powerful dictators are not dim-witted. Rather, they understand the check an armed citizenry gives its governmental officials. To disarm is to rule with complete power!

This is an easily understood principle. It is understood by the most elementary among us. So why then do gun control laws get passed by a very people who need them for the preservation of liberty? The answer is one word; 'Reasonable.' By using this declaration, politicians and anti-gunners alike can and do work on the emotions of the electorate to blind their more sensible and logical arguments. Who is going to say "no" to reasonable gun laws? If you do not pass reasonable measures, you are obviously not reasonable. Who wants to be seen as unreasonable?

The bottom line is this—no gun control law is reasonable. As the bumper sticker proclaims, "Guns don't kill people—people do." Gun control laws are simply a consequence of government mistrust of the people. Almost any item (a car, a knife, a rope, a plastic bag, bare hands, etc.) can be used to kill another human being. There are times when such killing is prudent and justified. There are other times when such killing is malicious and evil. The key is in punishing the crime rather than banning the various instruments that may be used.

JUSTIFIED BEFORE GOD

"You have rights antecedent to all earthly governments; rights that

cannot be repealed or restrained by human laws; rights derived from the Great Legislator of the Universe." —John Adams

In practice, you may be justified in certain circumstances before God, but at the very same time seen as a dissident before the law. Not all laws are moral. This principle is not just true on the broad sense, but in individual lives as well. For example, in many states it is illegal to drive a car without a seatbelt or while talking on a cell phone. Some states disallow citizens from carrying a concealed weapon without a permit or in carrying them at all. In each of these cases, to disobey would be a violation of governmental law. One would be hard-pressed, however, to articulate how not wearing your seatbelt would be in defiance of God's law. Indeed, one may find himself guilty and sent to jail in some cases, only to walk through the pearly gates of heaven without so much as a second look from St. Peter.

It is a precarious situation to find oneself, but one in which many have ultimately arrived. Natural Law—or God's Law—is the supreme law of the land. In the ideal circumstance, governmental laws are in accordance with and compliment Natural Laws. In reality, however, this is rarely the case.

Prudence would show that a certain amount of governmental law in opposition to the Creator's law is sustainable. Though living reasonably in society would dictate a certain amount of acceptance of such, the dichotomy can only be endured to a point.

DEFENSE IN LESS-SUBTLE WAYS

"Nonviolence is not to be used ever as the shield of the coward. It is the weapon of the brave." —Mohandas K. Gandhi

Though we may think and speak in terms of ultimate, life-altering/ending terms, there are, of course, many other ways that our unalienable rights can and should be defended. Most of us will not be called upon to pledge our lives in the defense of these rights. Rather, it is our right—yea, our duty—to defend them at other costs.

These costs may include our time, our money, our talents, our resources, our creativity, our status in the community, our jobs, our friendships, and even our family relationships if needs be (*KJV* Matt 12:46).

Indeed, though the ultimate price may be asked of us, it will likely not come in the same fashion. It would be well to remember that of the pledges the Signers of the *Declaration of Independence* committed (lives, fortunes, and sacred honor). Of those three commitments, only one of them was 'lives.'

Despite the hurdles, we must be involved in the defense of Natural Law. But, what can we do? What can we do, indeed. Go to town hall, county commission, city council and school board meetings! Speak up to your neighbors, friends, and family members! Protest! Write a controversial letter to the editor! Vote! Stand up and be heard for goodness sake!

It has been said that it is easy to lay down your life for a cause you believe in. The real question of integrity comes in the way you LIVE for the causes you espouse. Next time you overhear a conversation where principles are being violated, speak up! Next time those principles are being violated in your school district, neighborhood, or congressional district, do something about it. You may lose everything that is dear to you, but you will always be justified before your Maker.

CONCLUSION

"One loves to possess arms, though they hope never to have occasion for them." —Thomas Jefferson

It is important to understand—regarding this subject—that neither an avocation of civil disobedience or vigilante justice is being promoted here. In most cases, it is far better to "...suffer, while evils are sufferable..." (*Declaration of Independence*). Obey the laws of the land. Be a good citizen. Do not draw undo attention to yourself for a premature, non-consequential issue. However, there comes a point that it becomes "...their right...their duty, to throw off such government, and to provide new guards for their future security." (ibid). There may be time when you decide upon which mountain you take your stand. Be prepared for that day, but do not die on a mole-hill in the meantime.

The actual line that must be crossed is not one that can be defined here. It is a decision that one (or a group of several) must make before their Maker. However, some guidance on this issue is sensible.

Though requiring a man to disarm when entering a public school is clearly an abuse of governmental power, it is hardly reason enough (on its own) to justify war with that same government. The list of royal abuses Jefferson compiled in the *Declaration of Independence* was twenty-seven in length! The abuses had been ongoing for a number of years. Indeed, a rush to rebel was not reality. Sometimes prudence is the ally of virtue.

Likewise, though man may be justified in the sight of God, while at the same time being condemned in the sight of the mortal law, defending those rights may in fact require discretion. One should be careful to distinguish between unalienable rights and personal preferences. As outlined, unalienable rights are those given from the Creator himself. Though defense of any unalienable right would be justified before God, the way one does so may not be. Those which directly affect one's life, liberty, or property are the golden standard to which armed defiance might be measured.

CHAPTER VII

❧

To ensure freedom, the law must be created by a moral and educated people.

"Religion, morality, and knowledge being necessary to good government, and the happiness of mankind, schools and the means of education shall forever be encouraged."
—Northwest Ordinance, Article 3, 1787

INTRODUCTION

"The original Constitution was a dream that never came true... The genius of the Constitution shines when it is governing the right kind of people." —Dr. W. Cleon Skousen

Constitutional law is designed specifically for the purpose of governing, a self-governing type of people. They must be a knowledgeable and righteous people. The structure will work—for a time—on a lesser people, but will eventually be corrupted and manipulated into an almost alien concept.

Due in part to the simplicity of the United States *Constitution*, it has withstood the heat for over two centuries. A larger, more complex document may not have been as strong. However, it is currently being attacked, desecrated, and dismantled at an increasingly alarming rate.

It can be saved, but only by a people who are students of history and live by higher mores than the typical American television watcher.

ENSURING FREEDOM

"Whatever may be conceded to the influence of refined education on minds of peculiar structure, reason and experience both forbid us to expect that national morality can prevail in exclusion of religious principle." —George Washington

It is not the government's job to ensure freedom—only to help protect it. Liberty must ultimately be an individual choice. It is individuals, however, who create the laws for the whole. Thus, if our foundation is sound, the law, which is created by that same base of individuals, will also be sound.

In a Representative Republic, it is the few, elected by the many, which stand for and make decisions vicariously for their constituents. In general, 'the people' can be less than ideal in intelligence and moral structure and still enjoy good government, if those they elect are of a higher ethical and educational standing. It stands to reason, however, that this would not be the case for long if the majority of the people are corrupt. Eventually, their elected officials—as representatives of the people—would tend to reflect those who put them there.

It is essential for liberty to thrive that those who write, vote upon, and enact laws are living by correct principles. Freedom will most likely be ensured through representatives who have a knowledge of good government and history coupled with an above-average morality base.

LAW IS CREATED BY MEN

"When law and morality contradict each other, the citizen has the cruel alternative of either losing his moral sense or losing his respect for the law." —Frederic Bastiat

It is easy to fall into the trap of assuming that law and morality are similar if not equal animals. "Is that honest?" one might ask. An answer of, "Well, it's lawful," should not equate the two. The bottom line is that laws are made by politicians. Politicians are just people. People often make bad laws.

Remember the proper order of things. God creates man. Man creates government. Government writes laws—but only by the authority of men. Thus, if the authority figure is 'the people' and 'the people's' moral compass is pointed south, it stands to reason that there can, and are, immoral and unprincipled laws written. The fact is, when you check the laws that are proposed, written, or on the books these days, you find that the majority of them are in violation of one or more of *The 12 Principles of Liberty*™. In fact, most of them break Principle #3 for the mere fact that they even exist!

MORALITY

"Our Constitution was made only for a moral and religious people. It is wholly inadequate to the government of any other."
—John Adams

Regardless of how they may be painted by some, agenda driven, historians, the Founding Fathers were men of high moral integrity. They had to be in order that they might be in positions where they could be used as an instrument in God's hand to produce what they did. They were not faultless. They made their mistakes (some of them quite glaring) and even had some bad ideas, but they were men—in the end—who loved God, freedom and country. Furthermore, they were men who understood the position of morality in government.

Why should morality have anything at all to do with governing a people? How many times have you heard the mantra, 'But that is personal and private! His private life should have nothing to do with the way he will govern?' It is God who ultimately controls the destiny of nations. To be more correct—it is men who control their own destinies based upon heavenly laws that are created and enforced by God himself. If our virtue or morality is wrong, our lives will eventually go wrong. This is true for a collective people as well as for the individual.

The foundation of this nation was established on principles or righteousness. It was Benjamin Franklin who taught us that a moral people are the only people who can handle liberty. More and more regulation is needed the further society slips into evil. (Smyth, *The Writings of Benjamin Franklin*, 9:569). He was also cognizant of what could happen, even to a country with a well-written constitution, if the people eventually dwindled in corruption. Of the United States *Constitution*, he was heard prophesying that it would not be surprising to find that, after a few years of Constitutional government, it would eventually end in despotism. His reasoning for such pessimism? Corruption. (Benjamin Franklin, *Speech to Constitutional Convention*, 28 June 1787).

The question is thus begged, "Why try to save the *Constitution* and live righteously when the majority of those around us are unethical and immoral?" The answer is found in looking at how we got here in the first place. It did not happen overnight and it will not be solved overnight. Just as each individual helps to make up and impact the whole, your personal morality will have influence on the ethical standards of those you rub shoulders with and thus, the collective. That being said, it would be dishonest to not state the obvious. We, as a people, have travelled a great distance down the proverbial rabbit hole of corruption in the past few decades, but we have even further to go. As a matter of biblical prophecy, "see that ye be not troubled: for all these things must come to pass, but the end is not yet." (*KJV* Matt. 24:6). It will get worse before it gets better.

> "Can the Constitution work in twentieth-century [or, even worse, twenty-first century] America—with soaring crime rates, rampant disregard for law, tax evasion, unreliable promises, common place infidelity and immorality, with divorce and abortion as easy solutions?"
>
> "The constitutional republic can be secure only when there is renewed

respect for law and order, and for those who are responsible for keeping the peace; when the sacredness of all written or spoken contractual obligations is recognized; when parents and schools again teach sexual abstinence prior to marriage as the primary solution to problems such as unwanted pregnancy and sexually transmitted disease; when the right to life is preserved for all, including the unborn; when religion regains respect as the central source of all true morality." (John Eidsmoe, Christianity and the Constitution, page 381).

"Christians have a vital contribution to make to the health and well-being of America. They are needed to articulate biblical principles of government in every courtroom, legislative hall, and precinct meeting in the nation.

"Christians are needed to reestablish the moral tone of society... [they] must supply the moral fiber that comes from obedience to God and his natural and revealed laws if America is to survive as a free society. (ibid 410-11).

The fact that we, alone, may not be able to change the nation as a whole should not stop us from doing what is right and encouraging those around us to do the same. Often, it is about the difference we can make in our own sphere (which, in turn, affects the whole).

Start where you are. Begin with yourself, your family, your neighborhood, your community, etc. You can decide to be good. Your example will affect the choices of those in your sphere of influence. Stephen R. Covey talks about 'Circle of Concern' and 'Circle of Influence.' Your Circle of Concern is that which you can have little or no control over (the weather, the national debt, wars, etc.). Your focus should be on those things you do have control over, your Circle of Influence (your health, your family, your work environment, etc.) In other words, stand where you are planted and have an effect upon those to whom your life touches. (Covey, The 7 Habits of Highly Effective People, Principle I). Though times are tough (and, as prophesied, will get tougher) the difference you can make to the well-being of your immediate concerns can be measured. If enough are doing the same things, the difference it can make to the whole will be monumental.

THE PLACE OF GOVERNMENT IN RELIGION

> *"It will be recalled that Jefferson and Madison were anxious that the states intervene in religious matters so as to provide for equality among all religions, and that all churches or religions assigned preferential treatment should be disestablished from such prefer-ment. They further joined with the other Founders in expressing an anxiety that ALL religions be encouraged in order to promote the moral fiber and religious tone of the people. This, of course, would be impossible if there were an impenetrable 'wall' between church and state on the state level. Jefferson's 'wall' was obviously intended only for the federal government." —Dallin Harris Oaks*

It has become popular among some in this country to cry foul whenever the topic of God, religion, or morality is brought up in connection with government. "Separation of church and state! Separation of church and state!" they yell. It is interesting to note that a careful reading of the *Declaration of Independence*, Constitution, *Bill of Rights*, and all other Amendments reveals no such phrase as 'separation of church and state.' Rather, any casual perusal of the early founding papers, journals of the Framers, inscriptions on historical landmarks, and even our monetary coinage would reveal that quite the opposite is the case. Indeed, it was not until Jefferson was President in 1802 that the phrase even appeared, and his meaning was obviously not intended in the manner in which it is portrayed today. (See Dr. W. Cleon Skousen, The 5,000 Year Leap, 89). It should be remembered that, at the time, Jefferson was speaking from a federal—not state—governmental position.

God has historically been a major force on which the government of the United States of America has rested. Why then is there so much opposition to the role of religion within the state structure. Furthermore, why do so many claim that it was the Founders themselves who set up that wall of separation. The answer to this question stems from a confusion (either intentional or not) in what the Founders meant when they tried to keep religion and law on opposite sides of the bus. Remember, the Framers of our Constitution had just experienced first-hand what an oppressive monarchy could do to a people. They knew political leaders could have the most influence over a people if they used the emotions and dictates of religion as an instrument. A major force in their oppression was through the official religion of Great Britain—The Church of England. The Founders wanted to avoid all possibility of a State-endorsed or State-run religion. The 'separation' was thus a cry against State-endorsed religion (like England's), rather than a cry against religious influence on government all together.

In fact, the Founders of the Nation wanted, and understood inherently, the role religion must play in not only in the founding, but in sustaining the republic far into the future. In his Farewell Address, George Washington explained that a country's morality in general would die if it were not for religion. Indeed, it is virtue from which good government must grow.

A foreigner, Alexis de Tocqueville, after touring the new America wrote of the importance religion played in its success. "The Americans combine the notions of Christianity and of liberty so intimately in their minds, that it is impossible to make them conceive the one without the other...They brought with them into the New World a form of Christianity which I cannot better describe than by styling it a democratic and republican religion." (Democracy in America, 1:311)

Furthermore, it was not a national religion, but a merging of many sects which added to its success. "The sects that exist in the United States are innumerable. They all differ in respect to the worship which is due to the Creator; but they all agree in respect to the duties which are due from man to man.

"Clearly, religion is an important, yes even vital, part of our national

> *fabric. For it is religion which instills morality. "Let it simply be asked: Where is the security for property, for reputation, for life, if the sense of religious obligation desert the oaths which are the instruments of investigation in courts of justice? And let us with caution indulge the supposition that morality can be maintained without religion." (ibid p. 314)*

EDUCATION

"If a nation expects to be ignorant and free, in a state of civilization, it expects what never was and never will be." —Thomas Jefferson

When it comes to education, the Founders were no flunkies. Indeed, they were men of wisdom and well-versed in history, science, religion, mathematics, language, etc. Furthermore, they recognized the value of an educated people for the success of the nation.

Jefferson was one of the foremost educated among them and was an avid cheerleader for the education of the all citizens. He had every right to advocate for such utopia as he was a true scholar of history and civilizations. Indeed, he may have known more about the rise and fall of previous governments than any other of the Founding Fathers. He was tireless in his encouragement for an educated populace. To Jefferson, it was not reasonable or desirable that the people of America be educated. It was essential.

But, what is education? Clearly, when the Founders referred to knowledge, they were not talking about the number of certificates on one's wall. Formal education is important, yes, but self-education was their main modus-operandi. When Jefferson learned the Anglo-Saxon language, it was not part of a master's degree requirement or for the purpose of earning any special recognition. He simply wanted to study this ancient culture in the original lexis. When Benjamin Franklin tied a key to the end of a kite, it was not for the purpose of earning his electricity merit badge. When these men wanted to know something, they did not Google™ it. They studied, experienced and learned it on their own. Their desire was that every American would do the same. In their minds, education was the necessary prerequisite to any form of leadership.

It is interesting to note the number of present-day Americans who will go to the polls with little if any knowledge of the candidates or issues at hand. They understand the importance of taking part in the election, but do not yet grasp the concept of informed voting. Yet, we live in the 'Information Age.' With the numerous and readily available sources for information these days, 'blind voting' should never be acceptable.

PUBLIC EDUCATION IN AMERICA

"Promote then, as an object of primary importance, institutions for the general diffusion of knowledge." —George Washington

More and more, patriot Americans are becoming discourage, fed-up, and even outraged by what is occurring in our public school system. Many are seeing the system as a process of 'dumbing down' students in preparation for the work force (but not in preparation for leadership or entrepreneurial roles). Consequently, parents are turning to private and home schooling more so than they have in over a century. But, how did the leaders of 1776 feel about public education? A casual reading of their words would seem to reveal that they were very much in favor of a public school option.

It was in New England that the public education faction began in America. In 1647, the Massachusetts lawmakers began requiring communities to begin setting up public grammar schools. In order to have "knowledge diffused generally throughout the whole body of the people" as Adams put it, they would teach the three R's along with the Bible (Dr. W. Cleon Skousen, *The 5,000 Year Leap*).

Said Adams of public schools, "Laws for the liberal education of youth, especially of the lower class of people, are so extremely wise and useful, that, to a humane and generous mind, no expense for this purpose would be thought extravagant." (John Adams, *Thoughts on*

Government). This is an oft-quoted phrase used by promoters of the current school system.

Again, on the surface, it would appear that, of the present situation, the Founders would be in support. A more careful reading of their words (and a knowledge of their backgrounds) would reveal something much different. First and foremost, the Founders did not believe in or promote a compulsory education. "Is it a right or a duty in society to take care of their infant members in opposition to the will of the parent? How far does this right and duty extend? --to guard the life of the infant, his property, his instruction, his morals? ... It is better to tolerate the rare instance of a parent refusing to let his child be educated, than to shock the common feelings and ideas by the forcible asportation and education of the infant against the will of the father." (*Thomas Jefferson: Note to Elementary School Act*, 1817. ME 17:423)

Secondly, a national educational system with a 'Secretary of Education' as a Presidential cabinet post is a shame to the Framer's legacy. The above quotes from Washington, Adams, and Jefferson in favor of public education were not in reference to education at the Federal level. Instead, education on the public stage has traditionally been a state stewardship (10th Amendment to the US Constitution). Nowhere is the school system found in the enumerated powers of the Constitution. Of this resolve, Tom Corwin, a Whig Secretary of the Treasury in his December 1850 report clarified, "Sovereignty is the will of the sovereign people, and government, which is a mere servant or trustee, can never be sovereign, for it wields designated powers only. The people might have a hundred governments, each with a specific power, without surrendering an atom of sovereignty. Sovereignty, being the will of the people, is spiritual and indivisible."

Do not misunderstand, the Framers were in favor of a strong school system. They believed the educational system to be an integral part of freedom. They even believed that, for some, there would be no cost involved. But, they believed that funding for such classrooms would come from private donations or LOCAL taxes. "Declare the county ipso facto divided into wards...put to their vote whether they will have a school established, and the most central and convenient place for it : get them to meet and build a log school-house, have a roll taken of the children who would attend it, and of those of them able to pay; these would probably be sufficient to support a common teacher, instructing, gratis, the few unable to pay. If there should be a deficiency, it would require too trifling a contribution from the county to be complained of, and especially as the whole county would participate, where necessary, in the same resource. Should the company, by its vote, decide that it would have no school, let them remain without one. The advantages of this proceeding would be, that it would become the duty of the wardens elected by the county to take an active part in pressing the introduction of schools, and to look out for tutors. If, however, it is intended that the State Government shall take this business into its own hands, and provide schools for every county, then, by all means, strike out this provision...I should never wish that it should be placed on a worse footing than the rest of the State" (Thomas Jefferson, *Letters* 1308).

Probably one the biggest concerns to the Founders, should they be allowed to see our status quo, would be the lack of most parental involvement in a child's education. Thomas Jefferson was a big believer in the education of children with direct family involvement and continued, "If it is believed that these elementary schools will be better managed by the governor and council, the commissioners of the literary fund, or any other general authority of the government, than by the parents within each ward, it is a belief against all experience." (ibid).

> "[T]he foundations of our National policy . . . [should] be laid in the pure and immutable principles of private morality."
> —George Washington

Finally, the Framers believed that religion should be as much a part of a child's public school experience as mathematics or reading. A religious leader, Billy Graham, reminded us that they did not intend to take God out of schools. Said he, "America's [F]ounding [F]athers did not intend to take religion out of education. Many of the nation's greatest universities were founded by evangelists and religious leaders; but many of these have lost the [Founder's] concept and become secular institutions. Because of this attitude, secular education is stumbling and floundering." Oh, how the pendulum has swung.

CONCLUSION

"Preach, my dear Sir, a crusade against ignorance; establish and improve the law for educating the common people. Let our countrymen know that the people alone can protect us against these evils." —Thomas Jefferson

Without God there would be no United States of America. It is He who establishes what is moral and what is not. He made it possible for this nation to be created and it is He who (based on our actions) will make the ultimate determination of our fate.

It has been said that if we do not know our past will be doomed to repeat it. Education is essential in the preservation of good governmental principles. They are not new. They have been taught and tried for all of history. Most of the experiments on principles have been done. They do not need retried. It is up to us individually—and as a nation—to adhere to and teach them to our prosperity or not. Our nation's future depends upon it.

CHAPTER VIII

Freedom can only be sustained through a representative republic.

"What have you given us, Sir?" Was reportedly asked of Benjamin Franklin as he left Independence Hall in 1787. His Answer? "A republic, Madam, if you can keep it."

INTRODUCTION

"There is no good government but what is republican."
—*John Adams*

It has been said that 'the essence of freedom is the proper limitation of government.' It was not coincidental then that the government, as established in the United States by the Founding Fathers, was set up in the very fashion that it was. Much study, many debates, numerous writings, and hours of contemplation went into making the final product. In the end, it still was not perfect for there is always a risk to be taken when you try to govern a group of fallible, mortal men. However, it was as close to perfect law as can be enjoyed; at least until the Savior comes again to rule and reign personally upon the earth. (Dr. W. Cleon Skousen, *The Majesty of God's Law*).

Some may argue that Principle #7 could have been worded differently. The word 'only' is indeed more absolute than was desired. In the end however, it was a balancing act between being concise and being completely accurate. To write the principle, 'Freedom could be sustained in a number of different ways if the people were righteous and were ruled by God, but in an imperfect world, a representative republic is best,' might be more accurate, but it just does not roll off the tongue the same. In an ideal world, the Lord God would be our king. He, in perfect, omniscient wisdom could rule the masses with indisputable judgment, love, and understanding. Those days are yet to come. For now however, we—as imperfect humans—must do the best we can. After much study of historical governments and ancient philosophers of societies including Aristotle, Cicero, Montesquieu and more, the Founders developed a representative republic. This was not happenstance.

WE DO NOT LIVE IN A DEMOCRACY

> *"It may be concluded that [pure democracies]…have ever been spectacles of turbulence and contention; have ever been found incompatible with personal security or the rights of property; and have in general been as short in their lives as they have been violent in their deaths." —James Madison*

Ask the typical, 'man on the street' what form of government we belong to and you are going to get the same answer a majority of the time; "A Democracy" they will state emphatically. This answer is not coincidental. It was purposefully orchestrated.

Dr. W. Cleon Skousen, in his classic work *The 5,000 Year Leap* describes a movement in the early twentieth-century; associated with 'Progressivism,' whose goal it was to push their socialist agenda on America. Due to the natural resistance to the word 'socialist,' the group, originally called the Intercollegiate Socialist Society, deceptively changed its name to 'The League for Industrial DEMOCRACY (emphasis mine).' In order to further their goals, the word 'democracy' was increasingly used in direct opposition to the way it has been defined in the dictionary for many years (*KJV* Isaiah 5:20). Both the media and public school textbook authors picked up on this definition and began to use the word to describe the governmental system in the United States. Despite meager efforts to stop the purposeful confusion, the words 'democracy' and 'republic' became ever more confused as meaning the same thing (pgs 155-158.)

Even the most astute among us today are deceived into using the term 'democracy' when describing America's government. Thankfully, our very pledge reminds us what and who we are '…and to the REPUBLIC for which it stands…' if we will but pay attention.

DANGERS OF A DEMOCRACY

"A democracy is nothing more than mob rule, where fifty-one percent of the people may take away the rights of the other forty-nine." —Thomas Jefferson

On its surface, a democracy sounds like the perfect type of government. Why wouldn't 'majority rule' be in everyone's best interest? After all, would not the majority of the people choose best the majority of the time? An analogy is helpful here.

Let's say you are a part of a group of five. You happen to be rich by contemporary measures. The other four are poor. In this scenario, let's say one of the four decides that it isn't fair that you should have so much more money than they. He proposes a scheme to take your money and distribute it equally between all five. In a democracy, a vote would be taken, you would likely be out-voted, and your money would be gone. After all, 'majority rules.' Though this situation is hypothetical, it is not far from what actually takes place—on a larger stage—in a true democracy.

Democracies have been tried and they have failed. The Greeks are an example. Each time it was tried, however, majority rule disintegrated into a few with power and that eventually led to despotism. Thus it is with most forms of government when you are dealing with less than perfect people.

The biggest selling point of a democracy is also its Achilles heel. In order for a democracy to be textbook perfect, it requires the involvement of all the people in the society. When a law is passed, it is voted on and approved by a majority. History has shown, however that eventually the people get involved in other things. Consequently, they do not take the time to study about or vote on every issue. Hence, the democracy begins to dissolve.

The Framers were unified in their fear of a pure democracy. They were students of history and history showed that pure democracies, in the end, were always short-lived.

THE ONLY SUSTAINING FORM OF GOVERNMENT

"This vast territory is occupied now by ten states and will soon be by twelve. Forty years since it contained only about one hundred and fifty thousand souls; while it now contains little short of five millions. At the close of this century, if no calamity intervenes, it will contain, probably, one hundred millions — a day which some of our children may live to see; and when fully peopled, may accommodate three hundred millions." —John Adams

There has been some (albeit limited) criticism of this particular principle. Cynics claim that there are many forms of government that could work under certain circumstances. The key to the correctness of the principle is the word 'sustaining.' Indeed, most any form of government (even no government at all) may work for a time and/or in certain, controlled situations.

A form of communism and socialism work pretty well in a family environment. Dad may make the money and mom may stay home and raises the children. Money and necessities are distributed equally depending upon individual needs. No decent husband and father would withhold food, shelter, and clothing based on another family member's level of contribution to the overall structure.

A dictatorship may be the most efficient form of societal government in a hospital trauma unit. When the doctor 'dictates' to the nurse to 'hand me the hemostats,' she had better comply—and in a hurry. There is no time for debate or a vote on the matter. The same is usually true on the battlefield.

As seen in Rome and Greece (though not true forms), a democracy never endures. Eventually, the people begin to vote themselves more and more power, money, and privilege. The majority eventually become corrupt and cannibalize themselves.

Even anarchy (no government at all) may work for a while. Typically, anarchies begin when the people get fed up with their current form of government (whatever that may be) and decide to 'throw the whole lot of 'em out.' Though 'freedom' from any governmental intervention may seem ideal, eventually necessity requires some form of law. Complete anarchy equates to complete 'hand to mouth' livelihood. If there is no law, there is not private property. There is no punishment for 'wrong-doing' except by the victim. Protection of shelter, food source, and way of life is a full-time job. Thus, a sheriff is eventually considered prudent that people may leave their homes and venture out to make a living. Thus, government—in some form—is again developed.

Though the United States, in March of 1789, was the first to ever really try representative republicanism—in its true form—the Founders understood that it was the only form of government that would last through the ages. The form of government the Framers were developing was not intended to be a 'here today, gone tomorrow' scenario.

THERE ARE ACTUALLY ONLY TWO TYPES OF GOVERNMENT

"If men were angels, no government would be necessary. If angels were to govern men, neither external nor internal controls on government would be necessary. In framing a government which is to be administered by men over men, the great difficulty lies in this: you must first enable the government to control the governed; and in the next place oblige it to control itself." —James Madison

Many believe that on a political spectrum, there is a right and left side. On the far right, you have fascism. On the far left—communism. Everything else is located somewhere in between those two extremes. The problem with this continuum is that it is not accurate. In reality, communism and fascism are on the same side of the stick—the governmental control side.

The Founders had a better yard stick. They measured politics on the scale from no government (anarchy) to total government (tyranny). The best form of government is the one that can balance those two—giving freedom to the people while at the same time providing protection from abuse. (Dr. W. Cleon Skousen, *The 5,000 Year Leap*).

Governmental forms can be broken down into the following five categories:

Monarchy	Oligarchy	Democracy	Republic	Anarchy
Rule by	*Rule by a*	*Rule by a*	*Rule by*	*Rule by*
ONE	FEW	MAJORITY	LAW	NO ONE

In reality, however, they can be melted down into even fewer; an Oligarchy and a Republic.

Monarchy is defined as ruled by an individual (usually considered royalty). However, because that one will always surround himself with several, elite councilors, who help rule, it is in actuality an oligarchy. A democracy and anarchy will always degrade into an oligarchy in the exact same fashion.

That leaves a republic and an oligarchy. In truth, all governmental forms fit under one of these two forms of law. Furthermore, a quick look at present and historical governments show, by far, an oligarchy is the most common form (*Oligarchy vs Republic* parts 1 and 2).

THE DANGERS OF A KING

"I was much an enemy to monarchies before I came to Europe. I am ten thousand times more so, since I have seen what they are. There is scarcely an evil known in these countries, which may not be traced to their king." —Thomas Jefferson

The Founders understood intimately the dangers inherent in having a king to rule over them. It was for this very reason that the revolution against England, and King James, was waged to begin with. Again, the Founders were students of history. They knew that there have been moments in history where kingship has worked. However, these are always short-lived and the exceptions rather than the rule.

As Lord Acton taught, "Absolute power corrupts absolutely." It is in the nature of nearly every man to, when given a little power, usurp more and use every means at his disposal to keep it. This is the Achilles heal of kingship.

Unless a king is 'one of them, (meaning, he labors with, lives with, and associates with the people), it is difficult, if not impossible, for him to rule with any sense of fairness. Thomas Paine recognized that the whole concept of a king was ridiculous. By his very nature, he is in a different class than those he serves. He does not understand them because he is not—nor ever has been—one of them. Yet, with this lack of experience, he is expected to pass laws that are supposedly in the common man's best interest (Paine, *Common Sense*).

Even during a long, hard-fought battle for independence from the op-

pressive throne of England, many Colonists were unbelievably ready to try Monarchy once again in the form of General George Washington. In May of 1782, Colonel Lewis Nicola sent a dispatch to General Washington detailing the difficulties the army found itself under. It was getting almost no support from Congress and their solution was to crown George Washington as the King of America!

"But the idea of having an American king was profoundly distasteful to Washington. It was a slap in the face to everything he had given his life and fortune to achieve. His reply to Nicola was stern and uncompromising: 'No occurrence in the course of the war has given me more painful sensations than your information of there being such ideas existing in the army,...and [these] I must view with abhorrence and reprehend with severity.' Such ideas, he continued, were 'big with the greatest mischiefs that can befall my country...You could not have found a person to whom your schemes are more disagreeable.' He then urged Nicola from the depths of his soul: 'If you have any regard for your country, concern for yourself or posterity, or respect for me,...banish these thoughts [of monarchy] from your mind, and never communicate, as from yourself or anyone else, a sentiment of the like nature.'" (The Real George Washington, 373).

The Framers were aware of these kingly ruins and wrote often of their evil. How could they feel any other way? As students of history and observers of their contemporary world, the harms of a king were evident—even in their own lives.

Despite its downfalls, the desire of the people for Monarchy appears to be common to history. For some reason, people look for one individual to whom they can look to for guidance, direction, and leadership. The idea of a king, in and of itself, is not necessarily a bad thing. Kings are typically chosen at a time when the people are generally living righteously and thus, choose a righteous man as their leader. In this scenario, kingship is often preferred and usually works. The problem is in the duration of such utopia. One of two things will likely happen. Either the present ruler will allow the power and station of the office to corrupt him, or the successor to the crown will.

> *"I think a people cannot be long free, nor ever happy, whose government is in one assembly. My reasons for this opinion are as follow:*
>
> 1. *"A single assembly is liable to all the vices, follies, and frailties of an individual; subject to fits of humor, starts of passion, flights of enthusiasm, partialities, or prejudice, and consequently productive of hasty results and absurd judgments. And all these errors ought to be corrected and defects supplied by some controlling power.*
>
> 2. *"A single assembly is apt to be avaricious, and in time will not scruple to exempt itself from burdens which it will lay, without compunction, on its constituents.*
>
> 3. *"A single assembly is apt to grow ambitious, and after a time will not hesitate to vote itself perpetual. . . ."*
> —(John Adams, Thoughts on Government.)

Despite this sound reasoning, sovereigns have not hesitated to 'try it out' anyway. This can come about for many reasons (not the least of which is by force). Though God would have His people be an amiable society, man will, if he lacks a moral code, seek selfish power/money grabs through the violation of principle if given the chance. This is true with most men and is true with most small groups of men as well. When government is concentrated in the few in power, government eventually serves those same few.

REPRESENTATIVE REPUBLIC

> *"In a large society, inhabiting an extensive country, it is impossible that the whole should assemble to make laws. The first necessary step, then, is to depute power from the many to a few of the most*

wise and good…The principal difficulty lies, and the greatest care should be employed, in constituting this representative assembly. It should be in miniature an exact portrait of the people at large. It should think, feel, reason, and act like them." -John Adams

We know that Madison "did not sit with the others during the [Constitutional] debates. Day after day, for six to seven hours, Madison sat at the front of the room with his back mostly turned to Washington so he could fact the delegates." (Labunski, *James Madison and the struggle for the Bill of Rights*) But, where did Thomas Jefferson and John Adams sit during the Constitutional Convention of 1787? Answer: In France and England respectively. Some are surprised to know that two of the most influential of the Founding Fathers were not even present during the debates and compromises that eventually led to the writing of the United States Constitution. It would be unfair to say, however, that they did not have an enormous influence upon the document. In fact, the 'Father of the Constitution,' James Madison was tutored heavily by Jefferson and nearly all of the delegates to the Convention had read Adam's *Thoughts on Government* written in the spring of 1776. If one reads this document, a sort of ghost blueprint of what would eventually become the final text of the Constitution can be easily deciphered.

As previously stated, in a highly populated society, direct democracy just does not work. Eventually, it will be necessary to elect others to advocate for the constituents. In one sense, a representative republic is a type of small letter "d" democracy—at least In the beginning of the voting process. It is the people, as a whole, who rightfully assemble to 'democratically' vote for their candidates. It is after this occurrence that they then step back and allow those representatives—with much direction and encouragement from their constituents—to then govern on their behalf (Dr. W. Cleon Skousen, *The Majesty of God's Law*). Once those officials are elected, democracy ends and republicanism begins.

In giving a hypothetical example of how an obscure colony might establish a government, Thomas Paine gives an informative description of why a representative republic works so well. If a small society is located in a secluded part of the world, other forms of direct governmental involvement might work. However, as the population increases, so does the lack of participation in the administration of laws. Whether it be time commitments, distance, or other concerns, it eventually becomes inconvenient or impossible for all to meet frequently to make and review laws. The need for advocates then becomes apparent. Wise people from among them would be chosen to represent their feelings to the governing body of the whole. With a surrogate, the colonist is then free to go about his work, play, or other time commitments without restraint. Because the representatives would return often to those persons who sent them, they would remain loyal to their constituents. By frequently choosing others to replace the representatives, each would remain faithful to their peers to whom they must eventually report – (Paine, Common Sense).

In the end, next to a perfect theocracy (God governing either in person or by direct revelation), a republic—based on representatives chosen from the people—is the form of government which will give the most freedom, work with utmost efficiency, and be most sustainable for the long term. This act of intricate balancing was finally achieved for the first time in history on September 17, 1787.

CONCLUSION

"I confess that there are several parts of this constitution which I do not at present approve, but I am not sure I shall never approve them: For having lived long, I have experienced many instances of being obliged by better information, or fuller consideration, to change opinions even on important subjects, which I once thought right, but found to be otherwise... In these sentiments, Sir, I agree to this Constitution with all its faults."

—Benjamin Franklin

In 1787, a group of good men went to a good place and spent a good amount of time developing a good document which set forth a good government. Good; yes, but not perfect. In the end, it was the one government which had the most likely chance of perpetuating freedom as far into the future as could be hoped.

You have, no doubt, heard the axiom, 'do not re-invent the wheel.' Of course, if the wheel had already been invented, yet you had no knowledge of it, you would have no choice but to re-invent it in order to build a workable ox-cart. Thankfully, the Framers were students of history and observers of contemporary governmental structures. Though no society had yet invented a perfect, governmental wheel, the Framers were able to piece together parts that worked and parts that did not to create the utopian wheel of republicanism. They obtained the hub of representatives from ancient Israel and the Anglo-Saxons, the spoke of democracy from Greece and Rome, the inner-tube of Natural Law from Cicero, and the tread of the separation of powers from Polybius (and later Montesquieu). There were other sources as well, but because of the time period in which they lived, they were able to have all of this knowledge at their very fingertips.

The fact that all of the Founders were born when they were, where they were, and with the resources they had was nothing short of a miracle instituted by Divine Providence. Their presence on the American Continent, during the Enlightenment era, at middle age (with the obvious exception of Franklin), and with the background, education and life experiences they had was a sensation. Because of this amazing chain of events precisely falling into place, the longest lasting governmental structure ever to be formed by man has been ours to enjoy for over 200 years!

CHAPTER IX

⁓⁘⁓

To prevent the abuse of power, government must be limited, local, checked and balanced.

"It is impossible to introduce into society a greater change and greater evil than this: the conversion of the law into an instrument of plunder."—Frederic Bastiat

INTRODUCTION

"Governments are instituted among men, deriving their just powers from the consent of the governed."
                                        –Declaration of Independence

Most would agree, that a government which seeks to assert itself to the point of encroachment upon one's liberties, is abusive in nature and in its form of governance. These are the very same individuals with the belief and philosophy that its ruling power must be limited in its scope. Their influence may also seek ways to prevent such outcomes within government from occurring in the first instance. In our day and age there are many who experience difficulties explaining these beliefs and rallying those to their cause with any level or degree of certainty on how this can be prevented, or perhaps reversed. One can draw to the conclusion that when a government is large in its power, it should be avoided as if it were a plague. Complete presence of government results and functions like a dictatorship; a totalitarian form where all actions become subjected and required to live under absolute subservience to the whims of those in ruling power. On the other side of the spectrum, we experience the anarchic form of rule, which is actuality, by definition, no rule or principle at all.

Consider the following observation, "Government is a necessary evil." Why anyone would hold to such a statement as an application of some sort of truth is staggering. Government is a system by which a nation is governed. This is far from evil. In the estimation of those who advocate for principle, government is a necessary absolute, though it must be controlled. There is no coincidence that our founding documents held to this very principle.

THE THREATS OF THE ABUSIVE POWER GOVERNMENT

"Government is not reason, it is not eloquence–it is force! Like fire, it is a dangerous servant and a fearful master."
—*George Washington*

When individuals in seats of power usurp their authority under the law, tyranny or despotism exists. Although those appointed and elected to their stations by the voice of the people do, have a moral responsibility to act in a manner that is best for their constituents, can in most cases, cause serious contention. Rather, let discussions of principle take place; discussions relating to the issue at hand. Also, let there be persuasion as opposed to the force and deception that abounds in any abusive government.

A tyrannical or dictatorial form of government begins with a ruler (or set of rulers) who seize power through unconstitutional or worse, forceful methods. Through this explanation, one can weigh our current governance by making their own determination regarding the events surrounding our day. There are many instances where our freedoms and liberties are being encroached upon through abuses in our Government. Many of our elected officials are found in an unfavorable light through the exposure of the media, and point in a most unfavorable direction. One instance that has drawn much attention has been the remarks made by a recent State Representative who reportedly said, "I will vote adamantly against the interests of my district if I actually think what I am doing is going to be helpful… I will vote against their opinion if I actually believe it will help them" (Rep. Eric Masa as reported in *The Washington Times Online*, August 16, 2009). This may be a picture of one in elected office exerting his authority over the people whom he is called to represent. Though a representative of the people should always vote on true principles (regardless of the constituent's opinion), this type of statement is most often made in regard to a decision that is purely passion driven. A better method would be to discuss this particular issue with his constituents and attempt to persuade them or allow him or her to represent their interests, based upon principle rather than emotion only.

With those in power and seeking to remain in power, there becomes the risk of the mass creation of laws and regulations for the purpose of limiting the freedoms of individual citizens. This is done in the name of creating a more *just* and *socially equal* society, and in the name of safety. This is shaky ground, for there are many who would certainly advocate for a host of laws and regulations in the name of keeping one secure. This then becomes our responsibility; to determine whether or not these new provisions in our laws cross the intangible line between freedom and bondage. The moment you become limited in your freedom to choose (if the choice does not affect the liberties of another), you can be certain this line has been crossed. Thus, law after law and provision after provision starts us upon the slippery slope to bondage. Only then, through great difficulty and our moral judgment, are we forced to determine the course necessary to reverse such encroachments upon our liberties.

Here is an example from one side of the spectrum. An individual is faced with a personal choice to purchase a passenger vehicle for his or her family. Understandably, there are fixed aspects of any particular vehicle that are accepted. Certain safety features are included within the vehicle itself. There have also been extensive safety tests done on the vehicle to help ensure the safety of the both the driver and all passengers. These safety features are regulated and predetermined before the vehicle goes into production. Failure to comply with the inclusion of these features puts the manufacturer in a position where stiff fines and penalties are imposed. Additionally, many states have adopted various forms of seat belt laws, which are intended to protect the individual in the event of a vehicle accident. While it is left up to the individual to decide if this law is a practice they will choose to adopt in their day-to-day lives, there may be consequences for failure to comply. One could call these laws restrictive and abusive in their design. Each individual can still make the choice to obey or not obey. Where regulations have been put in place to provide the means to comply with the law, one would face positive or negative consequences with either choice that was made, whether the law was in place or not. An individual's life could be saved through compliance with putting on a seatbelt. Quite the opposite is true due to neglect. In other words, the law—passed in the name of safety—is mute. Disobedience will bring far more serious consequences than a fine or jail-time, could ever provide. Here we can see a subtle form of balance between laws and regulation to preserve freedom, versus laws and regulation designed to curb and limit freedom.

On the other end of the spectrum, an abusive Government might mandate not only the wearing of a seatbelt, but even the type and model of car in which one is able to drive. The regulations imposed upon the manufacturer could be such as to regulate the distance the vehicle could travel from day-to-day, the emissions acceptable for a given region, and even so far as to the type of *unnecessary features* (those designed for convenience i.e., sunroof, high performance engine, audio system, cruise control, etc.) that are to be offered. A driver would not only have to comply with these regulations (by default of the manufacturer's compliance with the laws and regulations imposed upon them), but further still, may have to deal with an entirely different set of laws governing personal travel. We can witness even today with our current and previous administrations, where some of these very regulations are being proposed.

While this threat may seem minor or far-fetched, the principle is the very same. An abusive government can impose threats to individual freedom through unchecked power. It can accomplish this through direct laws that affect its citizenry or indirectly through excessive and far-reaching regulation on industries such as: agriculture, education, energy, housing, medicine, travel, and a host of others yet to be developed.

GOVERNMENTS MUST BE LIMITED FOR THEIR SUCCESS

"The powers delegated by the proposed Constitution to the federal government are few and defined. Those which are to remain in the State governments are numerous and infinite…. The powers reserved to the several States will extend to all the objects which, in the ordinary course of affairs, concern the lives, liberties, and properties of the people, and the internal order, improvement, and prosperity of the State." —James Madison

A limited Government, small in its regulation of the people, provides the greatest opportunity for its own survival, the strength of its nation, and for the freedom and happiness of those who are governed. This limited form strengthens the position of each citizen by allowing their innovation, creativity, and intellect to further the advancement of new technologies. A prosperous nation is a nation that thrives through individual efforts, not an ever-increasing government which imposes scores of regulations.

Our Founding Fathers understood this and diligently sought, to make each citizen aware of this principle and its implications. The Constitutional Convention held in Philadelphia, Pennsylvania from May to September of 1787, could be considered a debate of ideas concerning the governance of the United States of America as it then, was operating under the Articles of Confederation.

A WORD ABOUT TERM LIMITS

"During the Constitutional Convention there were several attempts to put limitations on the length of time a particular official could serve. In each case the proposal was rejected."
—Dr. W. Cleon Skousen

The debate over term limits has been ongoing from the foundations of this country. The Founders believed a leader's stint in office should be temporary, yet there were no term limits in the *Constitution* as it was originally written. It was not until many years later, that it was amended to apply term limits. This is because many of the Fathers of our nation believed that the limit of one's term, should be controlled by the voters and not by an arbitrary length of time.

George Washington laid the foundation. He was a popular man and his election to the seat as the first President of the United States was a foregone conclusion. His re-election four years later was likewise imminent. At the end of his second term in office, the people cried for him to serve more. Many wanted him to be *President for life,* it was their *love* for him that was pronounced in his popularity. It was his *love of country* that caused him to take the higher road and step down.

This pattern was followed by all succeeding Presidents until the 1930's and 40's with Franklin D. Roosevelt. It was then (in 1947) that the 22nd Amendment to the *Constitution* was passed, making two terms in office a mandate.

Should term limits be the rule? The fact remains In a representative republic, term limits by ballot are the rule. Any politician can be voted out at anytime (during an election) by their constituents. The focus ought to be on each politician and the job they may or may not be doing. Then organize the vote. If the leader is doing the job the people desire, leave them in. If not, *throw them out!*

SURVIVAL OCCURS AT A LOCAL LEVEL

"Peace, commerce, and honest friendship with all nations, en-

tangling alliance with none." —Thomas Jefferson

What should our foreign policy be? It depends. Though we live in a world where we go to war with this county or that, and justify our actions with reasonable platitudes, the Founders (once again) had it right.

It is always in the best interest of the United States of America to be friendly with its neighbors across the world. That does not mean we 'get in bed' with certain countries, and it should not mean we leave our soil to police the world's affairs. Washington was a strong advocate of maintaining good relationships across the globe. He taught in his Farewell Address that we are to be faithful and just with all countries. For him, a battle-hard warrior, peace was the ultimate aim. However, in the very same communiqué, he warned of the dangers inherent in becoming too close with those same sovereigns and taught that inappropriate relationships with foreign powers, brings slavery. It would be interesting to know what he might think of our current indebtedness to China.

Jefferson was also insistent that we be corrigible, and not intimate with foreign allies. He taught that treaties of any kind with any nation were to be avoided. It was these very contracts, in his mind, that caused future wars. He declared boldly and on numerous occasions, that we should never become entangled in relationships with other nations.

Some would argue that we are already entangled, and are involved in NAFTA, NATO, the U.N. etc. How could we possibly just divorce ourselves and cut off those ties . The short answer is, we cannot. As with any current policy that is in place that violates principle, we just begin to move in the right direction. "So far as we have already formed engagements, let them be fulfilled with perfect good faith. Here let us stop" (George Washington, *Farewell Address*).

On a domestic level, many are disgruntled with the current state of our government. But what do we do? What must occur for our Republic to regain its strength and remain strong into the future and step away from large government involvement and encroachments upon our liberties. Letters to a President are simply that, letters only. A Commander-in-Chief may indeed take the time to read even more than a few of the letters addressed to him. It is quite doubtful however, that anyone but a microscopic minority would receive any response serious enough to amount to more than a mere feeling of acknowledgement. No one individual with any one idea, can have a voice loud enough through the words of a simple letter as to cause sweeping changes within an governmental administration whose ideology is rigid, if not fixed. A single voice must be added to another, and yet another, until the voice that is to be heard is sufficiently strong enough that it demands attention.

In every city across America, local leaders meet at a regularly scheduled time and place to discuss the things of local importance: building ordinances, use of public funds, local issues involving its local citizens, etc. This is where accountability begins, this is where the survival of our Republic has its most powerful ally. City Council Meetings, Town Halls and the like, are the breeding ground for true success and control over any further abuse from the government as a whole. When citizens hold their local leaders accountable (based upon principle and not emotion only) then local leaders understand that they are part of a political process and will better recognize they are servants *of the people*. This is done because the people in those meetings are your neighbors, your friends, your church congregation, and your school patrons. Though a President of the United States may indeed ignore most of the letters received, it is more difficult to ignore the woman at the microphone in a school board meeting when you know you will see her each week behind the counter at the grocery store.

Local government officials, once it is firmly established that their constituents will hold them accountable, can then work together with the citizens to support and uphold these leaders at the county and state level. This idea of holding local leaders accountable in this very manner, was not foreign to the Founding Fathers who understood the impact of a small group of people assembled together. By taking into account what they learned through study of ancient civilizations they will realize our government was set up in such a fashion that individuals could assist their communities in self government, and leave the weightier matters to a larger branch of government.

It was the Anglo-Saxons that would organize into smaller groups, allowing everyone to have a voice that could be heard. Dividing into units of ten families, fifty, a hundred, then a thousand (each with an elected representative) every individual was more sure of their concerns being addressed, their voices being heard, and was better able to hold their governing leaders accountable. With the door now open to greater control over government, the people were freer, not fearful of usurpation of authority, and more secure in a true representative republic with local accountability in place.

WHY MUST THERE BE CHECKS AND BALANCES

> *"The accumulation of all powers legislative, executive and judiciary in the same hands, whether of one, a few or many, and whether hereditary, self appointed, or elective, may justly be pronounced the very definition of tyranny." —James Madison*

With all that has been addressed regarding government, and the keeping of local leaders accountable for their decisions with regards to those for whom they serve, we would do well to recognize the important ideas regarding the checks and balances within the government.

The idea of a balanced government was not hatched at the Constitutional Convention of 1787. Rather, the wisdom of such a setup had been thought and written about for many years previous to this time. The Founders were students of history, and government, and were knowledgeable on these matters. Through their studies of Polybius, Rome, and Montesquieu, the major players at the Convention were able to come to the table with knowledge, which made the process providentially streamlined.

The Founders were quite careful in their consideration of the functions of government. With the House and the Senate as the legislative branch, the Commander in Chief over the executive branch of the government, and the judicial as a defender of the *Constitution*, these three branches of the government work together, and are unable to function properly as an independent.

Furthermore, there was a fourth check, the one you do not read about in your eighth grade US Government book, the States. Originally, the states wielded much more oversight and power with regard to the federal government than they do now.

Before 1913 and the 17th Amendment, United States Senators were not elected directly by the people. Instead, the Legislators of each state would select those whom they wished to represent them at the federal level. In this manner, Senators (unlike Congressmen) answered to the states, not directly to the voters. Since 1913, state's rights have been eroded to the point that many people do not know or understand the power they once wielded.

The purpose behind the three branches of the federal government and the power of the states ultimately served to guard against any form of abuse against the people. Additionally the three branches, as established by the Founders within the *Constitution*, serve to check each other through their assigned powers.

Checks and Balances

Legislative Branch Powers
- *Checks upon the Executive*
  - *Impeachment power (House)*
  - *Trial of impeachments (Senate)*
  - *Selection of the President (House) and Vice President (Senate) in the case of no majority of electoral votes*
  - *May override Presidential vetoes*
  - *Senate approves departmental appointments*
  - *Senate approves treaties and ambassadors*
  - *Approval of replacement for Vice President*
  - *Power to declare war*
  - *Power to enact taxes and allocate funds*

- President must, from time-to-time, deliver a State of the Union address to
- Checks upon the Judiciary
  - Senate approves federal judges
  - Impeachment power (House)
  - Trial of impeachments (Senate)
  - Power to initiate constitutional amendments
  - Power to set courts inferior to the Supreme Court
  - Power to set jurisdiction of courts
  - Power to alter the size of the Supreme Court
- Checks on the Legislature - because it is bicameral (having two branches or chambers) the Legislative branch has a degree of self-checking.
  - Bills must be passed by both houses of Congress
  - House must originate revenue bills
  - Neither house may adjourn for more than three days without the consent of the other house
  - All journals are to be published

Executive Branch
- Checks on the Legislature
  - Veto powers
  - The Vice President is President of the Senate
  - Commander in chief of the military
  - Recess appointments
  - Emergency calling into session of one or both houses of Congress
  - May force adjournment when both houses cannot agree on adjournment
  - Compensation cannot be diminished
- Checks on the Judiciary
  - Power to appoint judges
  - Pardon power
- Checks on the Executive

> - Vice President and Cabinet can vote that the President is unable to discharge his duties
>
> Judicial Branch
>   - Checks on the Legislature
>   - Judicial review
>   - Seats are held on good behavior
>   - Compensation cannot be diminished
>   - Checks on the Executive
>   - Judicial review
>   - Chief Justice sits as President of the Senate during presidential impeachment
>
> Mount, Steve. " Constitutional Topic: Checks and Balances." US-Constitution.net. 30 Nov 2001. http://www.usconstitution.net/consttop_cnb.html (3 Dec 2001)

A WORD ABOUT POLITICAL PARTIES

"There is an opinion that parties in free countries are useful checks upon the administration of the government and serve to keep alive the spirit of liberty. This within certain limits is probably true; and in governments of a monarchical cast, patriotism may look with indulgence, if not with favor, upon the spirit of party. But in those of the popular character, in governments purely elective, it is a spirit not to be encouraged." —George Washington

It has been said, that one of the greatest systems that the Founders gave us, was the two party system. It is a nice epitaph, but would have vehemently been denied by the Framers. Indeed, they were against such a system. It is as though they were prophetic in their aversion to such a system, and has been written on the negatives of the two-party system in the United States. It cannot be denied that many of our problems and difficulties can be traced back to that—one party trying to, *one-up*, another.

Avoiding such a system is more than difficult. Even the most respected of the Founders became entangled in such a fight. It has in fact, been indicated that the election between Adams of the Federalists Party, and Jefferson of the Democratic-Republican Party in 1796 that it was one of the most partisan and bitter in American history. Much of that bitterness came as a result of differences in party platform, rather than differences between the politicians themselves.

Nevertheless, if we are to move in the right direction with regard to our freedoms and liberties here in the United States, we may need to consider the abolishment of the two-party system. This is not a call for legalized elimination of such parties (this would, violate principle), but the combining of voices, ideals, and patriotism into the running and electing of politicians based on their stance, rather than their tie to any one political force. Though, like any rhetoric, this is easier said than done. We must stop electing unprincipled people to office just because they have a "D" or an "R" behind their names. This is the lazy-man's way of voting and has lead to a lazy and apathetic nation.

CONCLUSION

> *"The will of man is not shattered, but softened, bent, and guided; men are seldom forced by it to act, but they are constantly restrained from acting. Such a power does not destroy, but it prevents existence; it does not tyrannize, but it compresses, enervates, extinguishes, and stupefies a people, till each nation is reduced to nothing better than a flock of timid and industrious animals, of which the government is the shepherd." —Alexis de Tocqueville*

A people, in order to preserve freedom and liberty, may risk all they hold dear if they fail to institute and implement certain *checks and balances* upon their government. So what must one do to preserve freedom? One must hold firm to the principles throughout the Constitution and *Declaration of Independence*. Sit across the table face-to-face with your local community leaders and hold them accountable. Your individual *checks and balances* upon your government is to know those in elected office. Discover if those elected are individuals of integrity who will uphold the Constitution. If upheld, the *checks and balances* woven throughout our founding documents will preserve our freedoms and liberties by preventing the abuse and usurpation of power. The limits imposed upon government, are as important as the freedom each man seeks to enjoy.

CHAPTER X

———— ❧ ————

All mankind are created equal before God, the law, and in the protection of their rights.

"That all men are born to equal rights is clear. Every being has a right to his own, as clear, as moral, as sacred, as any other being has...But to teach that all men are born with equal powers and faculties, to equal influence in society, to equal property and advantages through life, is as gross a fraud, as glaring an imposition on the credulity of the people, as ever was practiced."—John Adams

INTRODUCTION

"Though I have said 'That all men by nature are equal,' I cannot be supposed to understand all sorts of 'equality.'...the equality I there spoke of as proper to the business at hand, being that equal right that every man hath to his natural freedom, without being subjected to the will or authority of any other man."—John Locke

Rights; are they simply given and protected for those who live in, and are citizens of the United States of America? Or rather, are they extended to all of mankind? These are philosophically difficult questions for many to answer fully as they strike a very tightly stretched cord.

Before such inquiries can be answered, a more basic and fundamental question must be asked and satisfied. When speaking of these rights and their overall reach and application, is undoubtedly of which rights are we speaking too directly? Before you can define whether or not our rights apply only to each of us as U.S. citizens or to the whole of mankind, one must narrow the examination. Otherwise, such a broad question will inevitably produce an equally broad answer.

All mankind has been blessed with the right to life, to liberty, and to the pursuit of their happiness by the hand of Divine Providence. These are all rights we espouse and recognize as outlined within our sacred *Declaration of Independence*. Furthermore, we have, through our *U.S. Constitution*, vouchsafed the laws and moral code by which we would live to safeguard these universally bestowed rights. These rights could be considered man's first rights. By virtue of his creation, man is blessed with life. That life demands his personal liberty. His liberty is met in his pursuit of his own happiness. These first rights are, and forever will be, extended to all men irrespective of race, color, or creed. Yet, no other place on this earth can be found where a people could, and rightfully so, declare to the world that this land upon which we live is truly the *Land of the Free*. All mankind is blessed with the same rights we enjoy, but not all of these rights are recognized or protected in equal manner in any other part of this world we each share. This *Land of the Free* has adopted many other rights which, by default are an extension of those we recognize as unalienable. This is precisely what makes our country a beacon of light and hope unto the world. All people of all lands have had these very same first rights granted unto them by our Creator. Nevertheless, our Creator has allowed our agency, our own (and our leader's) interpretation and implementation of these rights, and will hold us accountable for the execution thereof.

Although each of these unalienable rights of which we fight so hard to protect and enjoy have been extended to all of man, it is the rulers throughout world that have deliberately sought to strip their subjects of the free exercise thereof. It has been through a series of laws, taxes, regulations, restrictions, and many other limiting factors enacted throughout history in various countries of the world, that evils have been utilized for the purposes of maintaining control. Often, in the very name of freedom and liberty, control and bondage are imposed. It should be understood that, though these rights have been suppressed in these cases, they have not been taken away. They cannot be. Each of us was born with these rights and each of us will die with these same rights. Though designing men will suppress our freedoms within these rights, the rights themselves can never be taken away.

CREATED EQUAL VS. CREATED TO HAVE EQUALLY

> *"Laissez Faire does not mean: let soulless mechanical forces operate. It means: let individuals choose how they want to cooperate in the social division of labor and let them determine what the entrepreneurs should produce. ... Laissez fair means: let the individual citizen, the much talked about common man, choose and act and do not force him to yield to a dictator." -Ludwig Von Mises*

Everyone is not created physically equal, neither are we afforded the very same circumstances in which we are to live. These physical differences or living conditions, are only of consequence to us if we choose to be governed by them. Our Maker has created perfect diversity in this world, as no two individuals are alike. No two individuals are equally motivated. No two individuals will see the world in which they live equally. No two individuals experience personal, physical, emotional, or mental desires equally. Deeper still, while these are considered part of our human nature, they will never be experienced in an equal amount.

This world of diversity we live in is evidence that not every individual will achieve on the same level. Still, this contrast illustrates what one achieves through their own pursuit of happiness, provided they do not violate the rights of another, should be considered their own, as the fruits of their labor. Even a child would demonstrate this principle quite easily by answering a basic question, "If you work hard for something, and have been honest in your work, to who does it belong?" An interesting experiment would then be to ask the same child the follow up question, "Why?" This will teach the questioner about the mind of a child and also emphasize clearly the pretended differences we have come to embrace as adults when we make the leap from childhood to adulthood. This is where we drift from true accountability for choices, to the statist universal where accountability for agency is nowhere to be seen or heard.

Consider placing identical twins in the very same room, with the same goal in mind, both having equal ability, talent, motivation, and desire to achieve. Now set these two out upon the same course, on the very same day and hour, to speak to the very same people using the exact same words. Even with each of these *equalizing* factors in mind, the results will not be the same. Let's probe further. Suppose these two individuals were women, and they were selling a product that appealed to the public generally. Each has an equal number of inventory items. These sisters both look, act, and sound the same. Knowing what each will say, and to whom it will be said, they each set out together walking the very same path to approach the very same potential customer. Let's further assume that they speak in unison to this customer to avoid one woman having the advantage over the other. The customer must first make the choice whether or not to make the purchase. If they choose to purchase, they must now decide whether to buy from one or the other. Unless every customer, each time chooses to purchase two of the very same items—one from each—the results and outcome of these sisters cannot be the very same. One would inevitably complete their task before the other. One would have reached their goal first and therefore, although created equal, even identical, the two will not have equally the same result. Surely, one could take this illustration to an even greater extreme and say that all customers, having been created equal, would react the same. Thus produce equal results by purchasing the same amount at the same time, from each of the women. Notwithstanding, even this extreme situation presents an even greater paradox; wouldn't then, all women have to be selling the very same thing to the very same customers at the exact same time, having the same inventory, talents, ability, and motivation? Would not these inventory items have to be of the exact same quality, produced in the exact same manner, in precisely the same amounts for all things to be considered equal? And what of those that produce such items? Would not their ability to be considered equal be out of balance to those who do not spend the time to produce, but to sell only? If all the women in this example are selling the inventory, who is it that is producing? Would it not then have to be that every man is working to create what is to be sold? Furthermore, if every man is producing every item that every woman is seeking to sell, who then, are the customers? Sound ridiculous? Now the point is made.

No two people, even under the same conditions, and with the same abilities, will accomplish and attain the very same outcome. Even if the goals are the very same. The reason for this is that the talents and abilities of each individual will be exercised differently based upon experience, desire, and innovation. The reactions and responses from those whom they associate with can never be controlled and predicted, thus affecting every outcome. How then is mankind created equal?

EQUAL BEFORE GOD

> *"All men are equal before God, but all men are not equal before men because the differences are obvious."*
> —*James Thomas Kruger*

As each country, community, or family is diverse in circumstance, the equality before God, is evident by nature of those rights upon which all mankind can agree. Namely, and most paramount is the right to life. This right to life can, only through its violation, be thwarted. Life can be taken by murder or abortion, and while one may choose to commit either, the *opportunity* to life is extended to all equally by God. It is man that is to be considered the violator of such an opportunity and right, for man will limit and hinder such a right through his agency.

Equal in the preservation of liberty and in the pursuit of happiness, is man's agency. It is the agency to choose what one will pursue, to determine in advance what will or will not be accomplished. Agency and innocence provides no room for entitlement. Again, the child's answer to the question proposed previously, "If you work hard for something, and have been honest in your work, to who does it belong?" And to add to the question by asking why may be answered as simply as "Because I have worked for it." It takes an adult, one who's once innocent view of the world has been tweaked and manipulated, that answers the very same question, in this manner. *"It is mine whether or not I worked for it because, I am entitled to it."*

Man must utilize those gifts and abilities together, with their own individual agency to create the life they choose to live. As this choice will never be equal for everyone, the outcome will, in similar fashion, not be equal. How then is man equal before God? It is He that has provided equally to man the opportunity for life, the agency to determine how it will be cared for and the recognition of the accountability that follows. Man lives, chooses, and then must live with the consequences that proceed from his choice. God does not provide equally the education man receives; yet He provides the mind with the ability to attain an education through study, experience, or both. He does not provide equally the home or environment in which one lives; yet provides the opportunity for one to determine for themselves what type of home it will be. God does not provide the job, car, income, or material wealth as pursued by mankind; yet He provides to man equally the agency by which these things are to be prioritized in one's life.

EQUAL BEFORE THE LAW

"In all criminal prosecutions, the accused shall enjoy the right to a speedy and public trial, by an impartial jury." –Eighth Amendment to the U.S. Constitution

While every country, community, and family has its own set of laws and values it purports to uphold and adhere to, each variance creates a set of obvious differences and thus a perceived inequality. This supposed imbalance takes no account for the fact that the implementation of such laws and values, however different among nations, communities, and families, should be equal to the citizens or members of each. Every man, woman, and child should be equal before the law within each country, community, and family where they exist. While the agency of man is always a factor, each individual as created by God, is blessed with an evident and unalienable right to life. It is man, however, who chooses or determines how that life is to be protected, governed, or enslaved as the case may be.

It is our Creator that has provided mankind with the ability to think, act, reason, and determine their own course of action. This ability to reason and conclude is necessary for the preservation of the rights God has given to man. However, God, in His infinite wisdom, does not seek to destroy the agency of man by determining beforehand the manner in which each man is to live. The world has a set of fundamental guidelines and rules by which God has commanded man to live. We recognize these as the *Ten Commandments*. All religious tenants have similar teachings. A study of scripture further recognizes other laws and guidelines God has given men and commanded that they should live. Yet, the choice to obey is still ultimately our decision to make. Although these are not given equal weight in each location or among each people, the principle is the very same. Consequences do follow every choice made, and accountability for each choice is inescapable. We are each accountable to Him based on the light and knowledge which we have been given.

Since it is God that has provided mankind his agency, it is man that chooses whether or not temporal laws are just and equitable for their own benefit as opposed to those who only seek to gain power. Laws and rules are set specifically so that mankind can coexist. The level of existence or the quality of that existence is not to be laid before Supreme Governance to determine or but rather to those whom have been selected to hold such responsibility. The enforcement of such laws is equal to everyone who is not deliberately seeking to evade responsibility and accountability. This places a great burden on those selected to create, and enforce the law.

The morality and education of mankind will likewise play an important part in determining what types of laws are created, their intended purpose, and in what manner they are to be enforced. Where one community may seek to enforce laws determining dress and appearance of its citizens, another community might consider such laws restrictive and impeding upon individual freedom, thus restricting the laws. One may choose to live in a community, and over time, decide to move to another. Thus, their agency causes them to be equally subject to the laws in which they choose to reside.

THE SLAVERY STAIN

"Politicians, news media, college professors and leftists of other stripes are selling us lies and propaganda. To lay the groundwork for their increasingly successful attack on our Constitution, they must demean and criticize its authors." —Walter E. Williams

One of the loudest complaints coming from the anti-freedom crowd, is regarding the hypocritical position of the Framers with regard to equal rights. "If they were so high and mighty about people being born equal, why did some of them, own slaves?" Both Thomas Jefferson and George Washington owned over 200 slaves to work the fields of Mt. Vernon and Monticello.

There are many facets to this question which cannot be fully explored in this section, but there are a few things that are worth pointing out. To do so, does not fully give justice to the topic, but does give us a few things to think about.

First, the time period we are speaking of is over 200 years ago. I can hear the screams now, "But, you said principles never change!" Indeed, they don't. We must point out the timing for two reasons. Primarily, we must understand that the history saved from that generation is sketchy at best. Though there are many writings from the Founder's day, their attitudes, mannerisms, and of course, their innermost yearnings of the heart, are left to some speculation. The fact that some of them owned slaves does not, nor can it, tell the whole story. Secondly, though principles are the same yesterday, today, and forever, light and knowledge of those principles are ever growing. Understanding the truths of God in the Eighteenth Century is different than it is in the Twenty-first. I would never advocate that the Founders did not understand slavery was wrong at its very core, but I would sponsor the thought that the degree of the immorality may have been blurred and was not as clear as it is for you and I today.

To argue that *everyone was doing it* is no more justification for wrongs committed in 1787, than it is for your teenager as an excuse in contemporary society. However, there is something to be said about the time in which we live as it relates to our degree of judgment by the Almighty. Human *ownership* and slavery was as customary in the 1700's, as W-2 employees are for business owners today. The Founding Fathers were typically well-to-do, land owners, and managed large enterprises. In their day, right or wrong, slavery was a part of their equation.

If there can be such a thing as a *kind slave owner*, Thomas Jefferson is first on the list. There is one historical moment told of Jefferson's slaves gathering to greet him as he returned home from an extended trip. "When the carriage was opened, they received him in their arms and bore him to the house, crowded around and kissing his hands and feet—some blubbering and crying, others laughing. It seemed impossible to satisfy their anxiety to touch and kiss the very earth which bore him" (Sarah N. Randolph, *The Domestic Life of Thomas Jefferson*). Jefferson owned over 200 slaves at one time. Despite this blight, he was an ardent resister of such practice. In fact, he thought it was a *crucial stain* on the American way of life and fought throughout his early political career to scrub its observation from society. Twice, as a lawmaker, he tried to emancipate the slaves and twice he failed (Allison, Maxfield, Cook, Skousen, *The Real Thomas Jefferson*). Regardless, slavery remained legal and widely practiced throughout his life. Furthermore, there is evidence that Jefferson would have freed his own slaves except 1) They would have been worse off as free beings, as they were unprepared to face the world without the *structure* (however arcane) they were used to and 2) It was actually illegal in Virginia to do so (manumission). Upon his death, Jefferson freed many slaves through his will, and others chose to remain at Monticello where they felt at home.

George Washington is often accused of being a *white Christian* and *slave owner*. In his defense…guilty. He was both. He became a slave owner when his father died in the 1740's. He owned slaves throughout his life and a lot has been written (some true and some not) regarding their treatment. What we do know is that, like Jefferson, Washington preached against slavery, petitioned for laws allowing the liberation of the slaves, and emancipated all slaves upon he and his wife's death (Parry, Allison, Skousen, *The Real George Washington*).

We are not making excuses for these men, though they should be honored and upheld as some of the choicest of God's instruments for their time, they were indeed, not perfect. Human flaws exist in all men, and slavery was certainly one of them for many of the Founders. It would be more effective to focus on the truths and principles they taught and left for us, than to spend time trying to dig up dirt and tarnish their characters. A memorable lesson is widely taught regarding who it is that should *cast the first stone* that all men should greatly consider.

The largest dividing issue between the delegates of the Constitutional Convention in the hot summer months of 1787 was the question regarding slavery. The dividing lines were clearly set between the North and the South on this pivotal issue. Since the land owners in the South felt they needed the slaves (who made up about 40 percent of the population), and the North looked at it as a moral depravity, a rift of large proportions was wedged. Rather than a moral debate, the question was more logistical. How should black men and women be counted in the census? A petty argument to be sure, but population meant votes, and votes meant political power. In what finally became known as the *three-fifths compromise*, a settlement was forged, at least for the time being. Many years later, our country would atone dearly, in a great *Civil War* for the years of moral decay. Black men and women were treated as property rather than principally based and equal, under the law.

EQUAL IN PROTECTION OF RIGHTS

"...our fathers brought forth on this continent, a new nation, conceived in Liberty, and dedicated to the proposition that all men are created equal. Now we are engaged in a great civil war, testing whether that nation, or any nation so conceived and so dedicated, can long endure... that this nation, under God, shall have a new birth of freedom -- and that government of the people, by the people, for the people, shall not perish from the earth."
—Abraham Lincoln

Men institute governments for the purpose of mankind. It is these governing bodies that provide those who are governed, an opportunity to enjoy a level of freedom that only laws can provide. Should one community set in place no laws to protect private property, who would leave their home knowing that their property could be susceptible to theft? Should a community not set as a priority the right to protect one's life? Would not the members of that community, strong as they may be find themselves vulnerable to those who are yet stronger? Who would seek to take life in order to claim power over the rest of the community? A basic structure of governance must be in place for all members within a community to be even remotely, considered equal.

Self-Governance requires an individual, with a moral code of values, to consistently examine themselves to insure that the one's rights are not violated by the actions of others. While this type of governance could easily be confused with no-governance at all, it is a far-cry from anarchy. No governance of any kind, holds respect for one's life, liberty, or pursuance of happiness. It is a contradiction that in an environment without government, respect would be fostered for the rights of another. Likewise, no governance provides a breeding ground for destruction of the whole. A country, community, or family faces irreparable harm if a pattern is followed by which the rights of any member can be violated by another without repercussion or accountability. Once a form of accountability is set in place, governance exists.

While every form of government is distinct in its aim, its form must provide an equal level of protection to those who are governed. Debates will always be present as to which form of government is most appropriate or beneficial. That question is not at the heart of this principle (rather Principle #7). The principle is simply that in any given community, where any form of government exists, there is an equal protection of rights provided. Those entrusted with the authority of governance, should not suppress these rights and hold those they govern as less than themselves. Even in countries where no formal government has been established, self-governance is at the very least, should provide equal protection for the rights of those within the community.

Lawlessness will be present to one degree or another, in any country, community, or family unit. Only a system of laws meant to protect (not restrict) the rights of its members, will provide the equal protection necessary for it to survive more than just a short period.

CONCLUSION

"In a state of nature all men are equal in their rights, but they are not equal in power;... This being the case, the institution of civil society is for the purpose of making an equalization of powers that shall be parallel to, and a guarantee of the equality of rights." —Thomas Paine

It is probably the most quoted, yet most misunderstood phrase in all of American History, "All men are created equal." The way Jefferson penned it versus the way it is widely understood in contemporary society, are polar opposites.

To be recognized as equally created before God, the law, and in protection of rights man must hold to a recognition of the Divine and set in place laws of governance that are solely meant to protect men from violating the rights of others. There is no other way to thrive. The law must be clear and the law must be understood by all, that they may use their agency to determine their level of adherence. When man chooses to discount or eliminate God, there is no moral reason for adhering to laws meant to protect, or keep from creating laws that will bind. This leads one to live in fear of being taken advantage of, abused, or placed in a position of servant to the master, and slave to the tyrant.

There will always be individuals who will cry foul and say, "I have been wronged by another!" If such is the case, a system of laws must be established that a people can feel they have some kind of recourse and justice in the matter. All mankind is created equal with opportunities to determine what they may. It is the Creator that has provided equally the agency of man for the purpose of such a determination. This ability to think and reason, is key in providing the equal protection of the unalienable rights. This equality has never been meant to provide for all equal substance and equal riches of the world. Mankind, by his own will, utilizing his own agency, pursuing his own desires which he chooses for himself, must accomplish this on his own. Through the Grace of God, many blessings, agency, and gifts are available to all mankind, and are to be utilized to pursue, preserve, and protect.

CHAPTER XI

─────── ✧ ───────

All mankind are created with the ability to choose and each have responsibility for their own agency.

"Liberty not only means that the individual has both the opportunity and the burden of choice; it also means that he must bear the consequences of his actions and will receive praise or blame for them. Liberty and responsibility are inseparable." —Friedrich A. Hayek

INTRODUCTION

"Liberty, according to my metaphysics, is an intellectual quality, an attribute that belongs not to fate nor chance. Neither possesses it, neither is capable of it. There is nothing moral or immoral in the idea of it. The definition of it is a self-determining power in an intellectual agent. It implies thought and choice and power; it can elect between objects, indifferent in point of morality, neither morally good nor morally evil." —John Adams

Man did not create himself or his own mind. Choice is an inescapable truth. Mankind is in a constant state of decision: left or right, yes or no, to act now or to act later, etc. The failure to do so is a choice. There are those men and women that would say the forces of nature act upon mankind creating certain circumstances. Thus, they can claim that personal responsibility for one's future condition is beyond our control, which is a fallacy perpetrated upon the mind of the one who believes this doctrine. It remains and will forever remain, man's choice of whether to be governed by those presupposed forces of nature, or whether to be stewards over their own condition and take personal responsibility and accountability for their agency. No true, principled, or moral individual will ever seek to pass off any amount of accountability for his or her choices upon another individual. To do so would be inherently foreign to nature and create an internal conflict.

This situation can in no way, be avoided. Even in the simple and fragile state of one whose mental capacity is diminished, a choice can be and always is made. No matter how large or small the choice, no matter how great or seemingly insignificant these choices may be for those whose ability has been restricted at birth or through accident and illness, they are of far greater importance in their own lives than we could ever fully understand. It is this illustration of children under such circumstances that the men and women of the *no account-ability* doctrine, will point to as examples, what about the child who was born with mental difficulties? They are proof that all men surely must be governed by circumstance. To such, I will debate that a child born without the mental capacity as you or I, still acts and chooses at the level and degree to which they are capable. They will choose to crawl, walk, or run. The choices may be small, but they will choose every moment of every day. The justification that these *abstainers of accountability* seek, by pointing to the life of a disabled child and somehow use them as an example of how mankind as a whole has some pretended *out* when it comes to responsibility, is deplorable. It is an indicator of how far we have come as a people. We have willingly demoted ourselves from the role of steward, to that of slave.

The difference between the man whose ability is found complete versus the child whose ability has been minimized through birth, accident, or illness should be plain to the eyes and evident in light of principle. A man must look to himself for his own livelihood; whereas a child looks to his or her parents for support and has reliance upon them for sustenance and life. A child can only take accountability to the level and degree to which they have been taught, or to the degree in which they understand their actions. An adult, on the other hand, cannot escape accountability and responsibility for their choices. They can only accept them fully and to the extent that they are accompanied by knowledge. The alternative is to intentionally seek to evade them by shifting the responsibility upon another. This is, the result of a prior choice which brings yet an additional set of consequences.

The bottom line is this, each of us has knowledge. Some have more than others, but the amount of knowledge we possess determines the level of accountability we hold. Though we may live in a world where accountability is unpopular, it can never, be avoided.

AGENCY

"Nobody can transfer to another more power than he has in himself, and nobody has an absolute arbitrary power over himself, or over any other, to destroy his own life, or take away the life or property of another." —John Locke

When Jefferson penned the *Declaration of Independence*, very few things were changed by the *Committee of Five*. One of the most glaring changes occurred in the second paragraph, "We hold these truths to be self-evident" was originally written as, "We hold these truths to be sacred and undeniable." Sacred. Undeniable. Two words that though related to *self evident*, certainly have a character of their own. Rights, like all things from our Heavenly Father, are to be held in awe, honor, and reverence. The most important gift given to us by God is that of agency. The ability to choose stands supreme above all gifts from heaven.

But, what is agency? First, let it be stated what it is not. Agency is not the choice between good and bad, right and wrong. I am not saying that one does not have the right or ability to choose between good and evil, we do. When talking about the choice between what is good and bad, I am talking about what is good or bad in the first person. Man may, make choices which will knowingly harm another. They will never, however choose between what is good or bad for themselves as far as their own knowledge is concerned. Do not interpolate what I am not saying. Man can, make choices which harm themselves or others. They may do so not knowing it will ultimately do them harm. However, they always and I repeat, always, do so based on what they believe is in their own self-interest. It is what is referred to as physiological egoism.

> *"A free society will not function or maintain itself unless its members regard it as a right that each individual occupy the position that results from his action and accept it as due to his own action."*
> —*Friedrich A. Hayek*

Allow me a few examples. A teenager may be enticed by a group of friends to steal a pornographic magazine from a store. The teenager may know that stealing is morally wrong. He may also understand that pornography is degrading and addicting. In other words, he may know that doing what is being asked of him is *bad*. He might even choose to comply with his friends, not because he thinks doing it will somehow make it right, but because he believes it is in his current self-interest to be accepted by his *friends*. One addicted to nicotine in cigarettes, may choose to continue smoking, not out of ignorance as to what it is doing to his/her body, but because they want the small high it gives in the present moment. On the extreme end, a suicide bomber may understand that what he/she is doing to innocent life is wrong, but chooses to pull the cord anyway, in the end we always choose our own self-interest.

But, what about the altruist? What about the self-sacrificial man or woman who gives all he/she has for the benefit of others? The law is effectual, even when the motivation is, selflessness. Do you not believe that Mother Teresa knew that what she was doing would bring both great joy in mortality and eternal bliss in the life to come? I am not trying to diminish what she (or others like her) have done in the sacrifice of their fellow beings, but to think they were not rewarded for such acts is foolhardy. All who give time, talents, resources, substance, or money, do so not just out of interest for the welfare of others, but ultimately out of self-interest.! There is a reason natural law makes one feel good for giving to others.

With the foundation laid, it should be known that deception is the ultimate offense. When one is deceived into thinking that they are making a choice between good and bad what they are choosing is not. Agency has been taken from them. If we will always use our agency to decide what we feel is best for ourselves, the only way to circumvent the system is through ignorance and deception. The con which makes that decision cloudy at best, and blind at worse, is a crime of morality.

There is two ways to take the agency of another. You can coerce them or you can deceive them. Physical force cannot change the decision you still have control over in your mind as Viktor Frankl's experience displayed in his work, *Man's Search for Meaning*. Deception is the worse of the two crimes. Another name for Satan is the Great Deceiver. He is a thief of the minds of men. Can there be a worse title?

MANKIND'S ABILITIES

> *"We, therefore, the Representatives of the United States of America, in General Congress, Assembled, appealing to the Supreme Judge of the world for the rectitude of our intentions, do, in the Name, and by Authority of the good People of these Colonies, solemnly publish and declare, that these United Colonies are, and of Right ought to be Free and Independent States...And for the support of this Declaration, with a firm reliance on the Protection of Divine Providence, we mutually pledge to each other our Lives, our Fortunes and our Scared Honor." —The Declaration of Independence*

The Founding Fathers understood deeply and personally the principles of choice and accountability. They understood and upheld the agency of mankind. Written within our sacred, founding documents is a clear illustration to such a fact. A close examination of the *Declara-*

tion of Independence will quickly display a concise and succinct set of ideas that are made plain, first through a choice. These men wanted freedom. They chose freedom and accepted their fates in pursuit of the sovereignty they sought. Beginning with the first sentence of the *Declaration of Independence* to the very last, they pledged lives, fortunes, and sacred honor. They were willing to give all for the goal they desired. No rational individual could argue that these men were making a very deliberate choice, and would accept full responsibility for the very choices they were making.

Those elected to represent the thirteen colonies in accordance with principle, established a *Constitution* for the United States, by first making a choice. As citizens of this nation, men and women are elected as representatives through our choice to be involved in the political process. To not be involved in any way is also a choice in apathy. What we cannot decide, however is the consequences of our choices, and the results of our apathy or the conditions that will follow unprincipled decisions. We then live under the rule of law our choices have dictated. One could state that they did not choose the current President or State Representative, whether Republican, Democrat, Independent or otherwise, but did you choose to inform those around you as to the most principally-based candidate? Likewise, did you choose to do so in a deliberate way, or was it as casual as the suggestion of a good movie or restaurant? We live with the results of our decisions every day, and must accept accountability for each and every one of them.

Mankind is on display each with day the ability to choose. While the choices that are made from day to day may be influenced by family, and close associates, mentors, media, Internet, education and the experiences of life, none of these outside influences is ultimately responsible for the decisions made; nor will they have to accept the accountability and outcome that inevitably will follow. An example would be where we choose to live. One can purchase a home based upon the recommendation of a close friend, and can even choose to ask about neighborhood. But, if the area is to one's disliking, who holds the ultimate responsibility for the choice made to purchase the home in the recommended neighborhood? One could chose a particular investment because of an advertisement in a magazine, radio ad, newspaper, Internet or even the recommendation of a trusted advisor. The investment could ultimately prove to be flawed, one that loses some or all of the initial capital, but who then holds ultimate responsibility? The *abstainers of accountability* would argue the advertiser or advisor has a social responsibility to provide accurate information and is somehow responsible. To those, whom was the responsibility to determine if the investment was appropriate? Where is the personal accountability for the individuals decision. It is time to *stand up,* and face the inevitable consequences which befall our choices.

The capacity to think and act varies from person to person, just like one's talents and abilities. The capacity to discern between what is right or principled and what is wrong or unprincipled, must be taught and learned. As this occurs, it leads one to experience continued growth and understanding. While this process takes place, man's capacity to think, reason, and act upon one's best judgment is in a state of progression; provided the individual is seeking to learn and understand. This increases one's capacity, and when the decisions and choices made are in line with principle, the ability to accept full responsibility for the outcome is made easier.

CHOICE AS RELATED TO CONSEQUENCE

"While we are free to choose our actions, we are not free to choose the consequences of our actions." —Stephen R. Covey

Though the word *consequence* is often used in a negative connotation, it is not necessarily always bad. A *consequence* is simply the *result* that follows an *action*. When you jump into a pool with your clothes on, you get wet. When you lift weights, you build muscle. When you study, you gain knowledge. Abortion is not a right, it is an attempt to avoid consequence. The right to choose was exercised when the decision to engage in intercourse was made. Thus it is with any decision. When choices are made, results will always follow.

Even decisions made in ignorance have consequences. "But I did not know what it would do" does not change the results after the pin is pulled on the live grenade. In this case, ignorance is not bliss.

As pointed out earlier, children rely entirely upon their parents in their beginning years. They are provided for in every way. Food, clothing, shelter, and all that a child needs emotionally to thrive is made readily available (should the parents be responsible individuals themselves). As the child matures they will interact with other children and be exposed to the varying degrees of ability, mankind is blessed with. The child begins to learn how to reason and grasps the beginnings of problem-solving.

Education becomes a factor early on. The child will choose to pay close attention to their studies or slack with little effort at all. As this child matures into adolescence, and is capable of greater accountability, decisions are made as to how to apply the education they are receiving in the workforce. They are largely influenced as to the type of employment they are seeking, based upon their school workloads, their social activities, the media they are enveloped by, and the type of work that is available to them. Commencement ceremonies offer a great array of choices to the newly independent and self-governing individual. Will one pursue a collegiate education, seek advancement in current employment, take a year or two off to *figure things out*, serve their church or country, receive technical or vocational schooling, or something else, entirely? Choice after choice is presented and the diligence and effort that one puts in following through on each choice, is largely determined by the patterns set during adolescence. The study habits and work ethic that will be made manifest, is often a direct result of the choices made at an early age, and will largely determine the success of the individual in each succeeding choice.

Economic, political, social, physical, and even familial conditions outside the control of the individual will inescapably effect the situation and condition the individual will find themselves in. It is this very condition that the true character of the individual is magnified as if under a microscope. Does the individual seek to absolve him or herself of the responsibility for determining their next course of action, or will they take control to the very best of their ability and work to innovate a solution? As James Allen has stated, "A man's mind may be likened to a garden, which may be intelligently cultivated or allowed to run wild; but whether cultivated or neglected, it must, and will, bring forth. If no useful seeds are put into it, then an abundance of useless weed-seeds will fall therein, and will continue to produce their kind" (James Allen, *As a Man Thinketh*).

How does one react and respond to the world around them? Whether through careless spending, inability, or unwillingness to live within one's means. The loss of employment through downsizing or due to a poor work ethic, or simply the advancement in technology rendering ones skills obsolete, many will find themselves in hard, financial circumstances. Will the individual in such a place run to governmental agencies for the financial support they find themselves in need of? Will an individual seek to blame the condition they find themselves in upon elected representatives, and the choices of the *political elite* (choices made while the constituent was apathetic to the political process, or only complaining to their television sets and finding themselves more and more frustrated)? Does he or she cry foul, for the perceived mistreatment because of their own sense that they are being treated as less of an individual, and pull the social, race, gender, sexual orientation, religion, wealth, education or profession card? Perhaps the individual will seek to blame their woes upon a health care system that has somehow failed them. They may do so without taking accountability for the many years of deliberate choices that led to own their poor health. They may cry that it is the responsibility of those within the community to now pick up the pieces and care for and provide the necessary medical treatment, despite the poor choices that preceded.

A principled individual seeks to hedge against such difficulties by always seeking to improve, guarding against events that are anything but unforeseeable. And while all difficulty can never entirely be avoided, it is the principled individual that makes their choice and lives with the consequences that will indeed follow. It is the principled person who makes sure there are enough life-boats for everyone before setting sail on the Titanic.

RESPONSIBILITY AND ACCOUNTABILITY TO SELF, FAMILY, AND THE COMMUNITY

"If every person has the right to defend—even by force—his person, his liberty, and his property, then it follows that a group of men have the right to organize and support a common force to protect these rights constantly. Thus the principle of collective right its reason for existing, its lawfulness is based on individual rights". —Frederic Bastiat

All of mankind is blessed with unalienable rights from our Creator. Each individual is equally blessed with the ability to perform according to their realization of their rights. Life brings with it responsibility as an individual, as a parent, and as a member of society or community. Where the rights of one are to be protected, so should the equal rights of another.

As it relates to family, a mother and father have the responsibility to care for and nurture their children. Within this family circle, the parents act as the governing body. They set the ground rules and pass their own legislation to what is acceptable within the walls of the home. If a child violates the rights of another family member, it becomes the responsibility of the parents to act as judge, jury, and enforcer of the rules or laws that have been established. These rules and laws are set early on, and the children are given very little leeway in determining if these rules are for their own best interest. This is due to the fact that children are young in their understanding and it is for their own protection that these rules and laws are set. As children mature, allowances are made for the reevaluation of these rules. When they come to an age of accountability, other boundaries may be set, and a greater share of responsibility for the choices made by the child will rest with them. This will continue as the parents strive to teach their children the principles they will utilize in the governing of their own individual lives, once the child determines it is time to move on and begin to take on full responsibility. This process creates a pattern—a standard for the rearing and raising of a family. Once children have moved away from home, and start out on their own, the responsibility of parenthood does not cease to exist. As part of a family, when one member encounters great difficulty, due to the own choices (which may now beyond their own ability to solve), the responsibility does not shift to governments. Family members should work together to assist the member that has encountered the difficulty. Parents, will always have a level of responsibility and accountability for their children.

Communities in many aspects, function like a large family. There are very critical differences relating to the governance of and involvement within a community and that of a family. While a community is made up of many families, a community can, establish a government and set apart those who would guard the rights of every member. Much of what parents would do for their children, a police force would do for the members of the community. Equally so, while one family cannot force their own rules upon members of another family, a police officer cannot force the laws of the community upon members of a completely different community. There is an obvious difference between parents and police officers of course. Parents are not paid monetarily for the responsibility they have taken upon themselves. Since an officer of the law is paid for their services they render, they have the right to leave their employ and no longer hold the responsibility of enforcing the laws and protecting the rights of those within the community. Mothers and fathers do not have that right. Also, individuals within the community, unlike a family, will cast votes as to who will represent them in the governing bodies they have set up. The accountability then, of those who are elected is to those who they represent, those who entrusted them with the responsibility in the first place.

When a member of the community encounters great difficulty, due to the choices they have made the responsibility should not simply shift to community governments or completely to family members. Instead, members of that individual's family, work together to assist the member that has encountered difficulty. The first responsibility rests with the individual, secondly with the family, next to their church, and finally to the immediate community, or neighborhood.

Never should the responsibility be with a government that does not personal responsibility for the one needing help. Those in the know, those who could see fraud if it were being perpetrated can, through their own agency choose to what degree they can assist. The agency of those choosing to help can have its greatest effect solely because it is voluntary. A community that seeks to provide all of the means for every member of the community beyond a voluntary system is destined to fail.

One could argue that in order for a society or community to thrive, systems must be in place to impose upon each member, the things necessary to be virtuous so that care can be provided for every member. A case could be made that by imposing such measures, everyone is equally cared for. No principled individual would willingly allow any form of forced virtue. To do so would go against the laws of nature and of nature's God. Let a man be accountable for his own choices, and let him take responsibility for his own agency.

CONCLUSION

"Freedom of choice is probably the most audacious experiment in creation—man's endowment with freedom of choice. No other creature on earth has such freedom. Everything else in the universe, everything, animate or inanimate, follows a pattern to which it is bound and from which it cannot escape. Only man is free to control himself or run uncontrolled, to pray or to curse, to become a saint or be a sinner." —Carlton Williams

Choice is a personal matter, and cannot be forced upon another individual. If one would attempt through the use of force, to choose for another, does the choice truly exist or is it simply a predetermined outcome? It is the Marxist ideology that will delude and deceive the individual into believing that his or her life is meant for the wellbeing of anyone other than him or herself. To subscribe to the idea that a man must choose the safety and security of his fellow man, before his own in the name of the *common good* is blind reason. In order to fulfill such a *noble idea*, government must take on the responsibility of the general welfare on behalf of all of its citizenry, and thus regulate and control every aspect of the lives of its citizens. Agency of man does not and cannot exist in this system.

A man, must be free to decide for himself what he will become, how he will accomplish such and for what purpose. With this choice, he must accept full responsibility for his choices, actions, and consequences (results) that follow. He must remain firm on the principle that he cannot shift the burden to another. Will this man fail in his endeavors? Perhaps. Yet he is free to try again, having learned from the experience, stronger, wiser, and even more prepared for what it is he wishes in the pursuit of his own happiness. Can you assist him? If you so choose. It must be your decision and you likewise must accept full responsibility for your own choices, actions and consequences that will follow. This is what makes the United States of America so wonderful, and the Creator's gifts of liberty and agency ever more precious.

CHAPTER XII

꧁ ❧

Prosperity occurs when free enterprise and private property exist with minimal government regulation and restrained debt.

"The utopian schemes of leveling [redistribution of wealth], and a community of goods, are as visionary and impracticable as those which vest all property in the Crown. [These ideas] are arbitrary, despotic, and, in our government, unconstitutional." —Samuel Adams

INTRODUCTION

"Our properties within our own territories [should not] be taxed or regulated by any power on earth but our own."
—Thomas Jefferson

One hot summer afternoon two siblings, we'll call their last name 'Sweet', decide that it would be an interesting experiment to sell some lemonade in front of their home. They wanted to earn money for the yearly family vacation to Disneyland™ just before the summer school break ends. They work together at the kitchen table with blank sheets of paper in hand to record their objectives and then decide what time of day will work best for their new venture. The business plan and first steps of entrepreneurialism have begun in these young minds. It is this same spirit of free enterprise that our beloved country was founded upon. The ability for an individual to determine for themselves their own destiny, is vital, not only in the preservation of freedom but also in the long-term success of any nation.

While the older sibling decides that she will be responsible for determining the size of their stand, and how many cups they have to sell to meet their desired goal, the other sibling is tasked with making the appropriate brightly-colored signage for their new storefront and also picking sufficient lemons from the tree they planted together just a few short years ago. You can almost hear them talking and reflecting on their business plan and what led to its formation, "I'm sure glad we planted that lemon tree. We are going to have no problem having enough lemons," says one. "Well, what's cool is that we have all the tools, wood, and nails we need to build a professional looking lemonade stand, and we both like to build stuff," is the excited response.

With their stand built, signs posted, prices set, and lemons picked, all that is left is the secret formula to the soon to be *most popular* lemonade in the neighborhood. Research is begun, to the best of their young ability. Number of ice cubes to quarts of water, along with the number of lemons to cups of sugar for the most refreshing cup possible. Our two young entrepreneurs are well on their way to their goal. Though it is not a Fortune 500, they are beginning to understand what it means to be in business in America.

Mom and Dad, the final obstacle (or opportunity as the case may be), are approached with the idea, business plan, and first cups of 'Sweet's Lemonade.' With impressed parents, final supplies of cups and pitchers are borrowed (for a small fee) and advice is given on work ethic and the importance of staying positive and confident in their ability and product. This information is positively received and opening day is set for noon the following morning.

With 'Sweet's Lemonade Stand' set up early, these anxious new business owners await the twelve o'clock hour. Customers begin rolling buy, occasionally stopping and making their purchases. One cup, five, eleven, then nineteen and now twenty-five cups later, find our entrepreneurs feeling good about themselves and well on their way. Suddenly, they are hit with a startling new twist. A city code enforcer, and presumed customer of 'Sweet's Lemonade,' informs the children that the new, thriving lemonade stand is now closed. "But why," they ask?

NO PERMIT
TO SELL!

Now, the story that has just been illustrated may seem too far-fetched to be reality. However, any simple Internet search illustrates the reality of this very experience. One such story in California has been the basic context for the very example that was used here. Children are having lemonade stands closed over ridiculous reasons. City Councils are regulating what is safe and what is not, what areas can be used for business and which are deemed unfit for commerce. Never mind the fact that these are lemons from their own trees, with sugar from their own pantry, ice cubes from their own freezer, and water from their own tap. Innovation has been halted, and the spirit of the free market threatened again with over-regulation.

What is it about the free market that scares individuals so much that regulation and ever-more regulation is welcomed? This type of overreach, causes the final product delivered from the production line to be a distant cousin of the original idea?

WHAT DETERMINES PROSPERITY?

"It is not from the benevolence of the butcher, the brewer, or the baker that we expect our dinner, but from their regard to their own interest. We address ourselves, not to their humanity but to their self-love." —Adam Smith

The Founders were not poor. Though some died in debt, this was typically due to leverage, rather than poor stewardship. In most contemporary men's opinions, they would be considered *prosperous*.

It is important to first note that the idea of prosperity can take on many different forms for every individual. Money or currency as a tangible affect of a successful endeavor, may be the definition of prosperity for one. For another, the ability to have the type of employment or working schedule that allows for more time with the family, can more accurately describe prosperity. Still, choosing and then working in a desired field of labor can be the ultimate aim, despite the amount of money or time with the family. Even the size and closeness of the family itself, could define prosperity. In all of these examples, along with many others, the answer is always the same. It is the individual that determines prosperity.

"From each according to his ability, to each according to his need" —Karl Marx

Given this understanding, it is essential that the individual using their own measure of prosperity, in conjunction with an understanding of unalienable rights, is afforded the ability to engage one's own mind and innovate for themselves that which they purport to bring them their own measure of prosperity. Without the basic understanding of how unalienable rights fit within this process, one could easily determine that in order to pursue prosperity, it would have to be done through the violation of another's rights. This, of course, cannot be the case. Additionally, a government entity, as set up by a culture or society of people for the express purpose of preserving these rights, could in fact determine that *in the best interest of the society*, the rights of an individual can be violated in the pursuit of collective prosperity. This is exactly the type of philosophy that leads to a Marxist Society. The idea that one could be sacrificed for the benefit of the collective is not only destructive in its nature, it cannot be self-sustaining. The society or culture ultimately destroys itself in the very guise of preservation.

A rational and logical understanding, and acceptance of unalienable rights, provides for all members of a culture or society an objective standard by which to measure how to pursue one's own self-interest in their search of prosperity. One must recognize that it is the utilization of the mind, with respect to rights and principles, that offer the opportunity to achieve prosperity.

HOW THE FREE ENTERPRISE SYSTEM WORKS RELATING TO PRIVATE PROPERTY?

"I cannot undertake to lay my finger on that article of the Constitution which granted a right to Congress of expending, on objects of benevolence, the money of their constituents." —James Madison

The free enterprise system is a structure by which individuals can offer and exchange goods or services freely amongst themselves. While this system is local in its infancy, the evolution of ideas, innovation, and further utilization of such a system creates an even greater opportunity to exchange beyond the confines of local geographical areas. A simple illustration is that of a local merchant who sells a specific product. While they may be limited physically, to their relatively small geographical area, the invention or innovation that led to the advancement in transportation, provides an even greater reach. Subsequently, further advancement in technology cannot only offer the opportunity for greater innovation to create the same product in a much more efficient manner, it could also present an even greater reach in customer base. This obviously affects the bottom line that has been seen most dramatically with the advent of the Internet.

While reading the Founder's historical writings, it is easy to misunderstand the term, "property." A contemporary meaning of the word is most often related singularly to real estate. This type of property ownership fits the principle, and it is not the only form of property. Property in this sense ranges from land, to possessions, to ideas or intellectual property. In a free society, all private ownership must be protected.

The manner in which the free enterprise system relates to private property is illustrated using the previous example of 'Sweet's Lemonade Stand.' It was the private property, (the lemons, sugar, materials for the stand, and other tangible elements) together with the innovation, (intellectual property) that led to the business plan and idea in the first instance. These elements could only be put to use to achieve true individual prosperity in a free exchange system. If we assert that the elements belonged to the individuals, and therefore as their own property, are free to be distributed and exchanged as they so choose. This is what is meant by private property within the free enterprise system.

EXCESSIVE GOVERNMENT REGULATION, AND ITS UNINTENDED CONSEQUENCES

"As to depressions and mass unemployment; they are not caused by the free market, but by government interference into the economy." —Ayn Rand

Regulation by definition, is a series of laws and boundaries as prescribed by authority to determine or control conduct. Regulation is not inherently bad or undesirable. In fact, we have established previously, that some degree of government regulation can be essential. All regulation, however, has unintended consequences. Therefore, we must define the parameters. What kind and how much regulation is acceptable? Who decides what types of regulation are desirable, and how are they enforced?

Those laws and boundaries which are most conducive to a free enterprise system are those which protect an individual from willful or deliberate harm or fraud. 'Sweet's Lemonade Stand' decides that it will sell its product to its customers. Let's assume that, in the interest of making the highest profit, Sweet's realizes that the oranges found on their property are more abundant than that of the lemons. Furthermore, the juice derived from these oranges is far greater than the juice of the lemons. The CEOs of 'Sweet's Lemonade Stand' now have a choice. If they decide to sell the juice of the orange, they can change their name and advertise with integrity, or they can lie to their customer base and sell orange juice disguised as lemonade. For this example, let's assume that 'Sweet's Lemonade Stand' chooses to deceive its customer base and intentionally practice the misrepresentation of their product. Here is where minimal and *proper* regulation could certainly play a role. Suppose Mr. Drymouth is thirsty and would like a lemonade. He makes a purchase, and (unbeknownst to the owners of Sweet's) Drymouth has an allergic reaction to the orange juice. We now have a clear case of misrepresentation. An individual who is knowingly allergic to orange juice would not have purchased such a product. The proper regulation in this instance is meant to require a disclosure to the customer regarding the nature of the product they are purchasing.

Let's assume even further that the orange tree is not truly on the property of the 'Sweet's Lemonade Stand' owners, but is instead growing on a neighboring property. The fruit of the tree is within picking distance as to allow for it to be harvested without having to enter or cross into the neighboring yard. Sweet's decides to not participate in a misrepresentation of the type of juice they are offering and change its name and advertising materials to support the sale of orange juice. While they are selling the very product they are claiming to offer, proper regulations would again play a role. To sell a product in this manner, violates basic regulations since Sweet's does not first own the oranges (nor have they given proper compensation to the true owner) they are using for their products.

As an answer to ever encroaching government control over the economy (Mercantilism), Adam Smith's classic An Inquiry into the Nature and Causes of the Wealth of Nations was published in 1776. Some would say it was in just the nick of time. Others understand the providential timing. In his study, Smith taught that in order to have a prosperous economy, the people should have freedom to try, freedom to buy, freedom to sell, and freedom to fail.

Smith also reminded the Founders that in order to allow the economy

> to work properly, government should, recues itself. Smith pointed out
> only four areas where government should be involved in economic
> policy in order to protect the integrity of the market. They are:
> 1. Prevent the use of force in the market place.
> 2. Prevent fraud.
> 3. Prevent monopoly of goods or resources.
> 4. Prevent the debauchery of society
> (Dr. W. Cleon Skousen, The Majesty of God's Law)

There are many who do not trust the free enterprise system of capitalism to do the right thing. Some say "there must be governmental oversight" they shout. How else can we trust the *fat-cats* who are stuffing their pockets to do that which is in the best interest of the consumer? The fact is, the free commerce system works as an unintended byproduct of the *fat cats* doing what is in their own best interest of the consumer. Their actions cause *all* to become rich and prosperous as better products and services are made cheaper. On the opposite side, extreme government regulation also creates unintended consequences. These consequences are visible all around us. Here is an example, speaking on the subject of the Food and Drug Association (FDA), and government regulation of pharmaceutical companies, Milton Friedman, American economist and Nobel Prize winner, pointed out how excessive regulation and pressure on the FDA pushes them to "always be late in approving [pharmaceutical drugs] and that there is enormous evidence that they [the FDA] have caused more deaths by late approvals than they have saved by early approvals." Addressing ineffective or dangerous drugs that could harm or perhaps kill individuals, Mr. Friedman states further, "that it is in the self interest of these pharmaceutical companies not to have these bad things happen." He is in effect arguing the case for self-regulation by the pharmaceutical companies themselves and not the FDA (*Take it to the limits: Milton Friedman on Libertarianism*, Recorded on Feb 10, 1999)

It becomes the responsibility of those within the free enterprise system, together with the regulating agencies within the government, to create a system of policies that offer full disclosure and recourse for misrepresentation and willful violation of basic regulations. Excessive regulation, stifles business and in effect, slows and halts progress. It provides an atmosphere where a business is laden with fines and permits to the degree that higher prices must be imposed upon the consumer. In the interest of protecting the consumer, regulatory bodies create the environment whereby unintended consequences occur. These consequences may include higher prices, lower wages, lower quality of product, or even the non-existence of a company and product that could otherwise be beneficial to all members of society.

IS IT POSSIBLE FOR THE FREE ENTERPRISE SYSTEM TO SELF REGULATE?

"The issue is always the same: the government or the market. There is no third solution." —Ludwig Van Mises

In both cases cited (namely 'Sweet's Lemonade Stand' and the pharmaceutical companies discussed by Mr. Friedman), the companies are motivated by their own self-interest to offer the best product, for the best price, without compromising their integrity and thus harming their consumers. Self-regulation within the free enterprise system happens more often than one might assume. The very fact that we live in an imposed regulation-ridden world, causes us to think that this is the natural way, indeed the only way society can survive.

In the case of Sweet's, would it not be in their self-interest to use only the ripest fruits and the cleanest water? Surely a bad fruit and dirty water does not make for a welcoming glass of lemonade on a hot summer afternoon. It would not take too many sick or disgusted customers before the word would start to spread throughout the neighborhood. Still, the selling of orange juice as lemonade or orange juice made from stolen property would quickly create a stir within the community that the product is *not as advertised*, and stigmatizing the small entrepreneurs as dishonest. This would lead to the closure of the business itself, as a fundamental principle of honesty and integrity would be found lacking.

The principle is not lost on the larger companies either. In the case of the pharmaceutical industry, as Mr. Friedman points out, who has greater self interest to provide the greatest drugs and medications, the company itself or the regulatory body designed to place and impose limits? In fact, in a crude dichotomy, a regulation today may actually cause a company to be less careful. They can always blame the agency for a failure, a faulty drug, or medication that does not provide full disclosure of side effects. Ingredients could very well result in death, though some would argue that the almighty dollar would, supersede morality, the bottom line is not lost on morality. It is in the very reason for being in business ,*the almighty dollar,* that the pharmaceutical companies will regulate themselves. To not do so, would quickly cause its own demise the very same as in the case of the two little girls above. It is in their best interest to regulate and disclose to the point that they inform the consumer to the best of their ability. If nothing else, they avoid lawsuits and repercussion from the legal system should an accidental death or any measure of harm occur. Within the same interview, Mr. Friedman gives another example to illustrate how self-regulation would take place within large companies of another industry, and in a voluntary manner by simply asking the question, "Who, has the most interest in preventing airline accidents?" (Milton Frideman, *Take it to the Limits* interview with Peter Robinson). Who indeed? Archie Bunker may have been on to something when he satirically opined that to prevent hijackings, the airlines ought to issue every passenger a gun as they board.

The Real Story of the First Thanksgiving

It is common practice among proud Americans to celebrate the Thanksgiving Holiday with a recounting of the story of the first Thanksgiving. Typically, the story is told that the pilgrims traveled to America in search of religious freedom. While here, they worked hard to build, plant, and survive, but had a difficult time. Due to the unfamiliar circumstances, they were unable to grow much food or find much game. Enter the Indians. Friendly Squanto and Samoset wander on from stage left and quickly make friends with the English settlers. Because of their great generosity, the Indians teach the white man how to plant corn (one dead fish per stock), shoot deer, and build a log cabin. The result is a bounteous harvest. In return for the hospitality shown, the white man holds a great feast with turkey, cranberry sauce, and stuffing. Of course, they then invite the Indians to join them. It is a great story to tell before we all indulge in gluttony each November. The problem is; the story is not true.

The actual story of the first few years in America for the settlers was quite a different one. Dr. W. Cleon Skousen, in The Majesty of God's Law, retells the writings of John Fiske, an early American historian, as he paints a much different picture in his Historical Writings. He tells the story of Jamestown as a business venture. Several English investors formed the London Company and pooled their resources to send a group to America and establish a settlement there. The purpose? Well, easy money.

"Those who came over with jubilant enthusiasm soon learned the terrible reality of seeing thousands dying from starvation while others were forced to beg for a few handful of corn from the Indians. Eventually, the newcomer became reconciled to the threatening dangers of life on the frontier and the price they had to pay to survive. It meant hard work from dawn to dusk, extremely careful preserving and storing of resources, living frugally, even austerely, and above all, keeping their powder dry and risking life itself at a moment's notice for the protection of life and love one from the tomahawks, raping and looking of wild savages."

The most difficult circumstances, did not come in the form of Indians or rugged land at all; they came in the form of bad government. Because the London Company was in control of the money, they were also in control of the government. Accordingly, they established the rules and laws in which the new settlers would live. Their choice of government? ...Voluntary (actually compulsory) communism.

"It did not take long to discover that human nature does not adapt itself to working voluntarily when it is known that all will share equally in the harvest whether they worked or not. Not only is this arrangement an open invitation for the lazy to engage in malingering, but those who actually do the work feel cheated when they see the lazy settlers getting as much as those who performed the labor."

Consequent to the lack of reward for productivity, the settlers suffered that first season. The original 105 people were reduced to a mere 38. "Finally–by 1611- the London Company realized it had made a terrible mistake by refusing to allow the settlers to have private property and operate on their own initiative. Sir Thomas Dale was sent..[and] under his direction communism was abandoned."

Fiske continues, "Six month after Dale's administration had begun, a fresh supply of settlers raised the whole number to nearly eight hundred and a good stock of cows, oxen, and goats were added to their resources. The colony now began to expand itself beyond the immediate neighborhood of Jamestown" (The historical writings of John Fiske).

When the Pilgrims came to America in 1620, and established a colony at Plymouth, they had not learned their history very well. Once again, the stockholders forced the people into a compulsory form of communism. Despite its predictable failure, there were enough men that, with the help of affable Indians, they were able to have a Thanksgiving Celebration at the end of the first season. Not long afterwards, the communistic, socialistic way of life was abandoned.

Governor William Bradford explained, "At last after much debate of things, the governor gave way that they should set corn everyman for his own particular... That had very good success for it made all hands very industrious, so much [more] corn was planted than otherwise *would have been by any means the Governor or any other could use, and saved him a great deal of trouble, and gave far better content. The women now went willingly into the field, and took their little-ones with them to set corn, which before would allege weakness, and inability; whom to have compelled would have been thought great tyranny and oppression. The experience that was had in this common course and condition, tried sundry years, and that amongst godly and sober men, may well evince the vanity of that conceit of Plato and other ancients, applauded by some of later times; that the taking away of property, and bringing in community into a commonwealth, would make them happy and flourishing; as if they were wiser than God"* (William Bradford, *Of Plymouth Plantation*).

Rush Limbaugh picks up there. "Now, other than on this [children's Thanksgiving] program every year, have you heard this story before? Is this lesson being taught to your kids today -- and if it isn't, why not? Can you think of a more important lesson one could derive from the pilgrim experience?"

"So in essence there was, thanks to the Indians, because they taught us how to skin beavers and how to plant corn when we arrived, but the real Thanksgiving was thanking the Lord for guidance and plenty -- and once they reformed their system and got rid of the communal bottle and started what was essentially free market capitalism, they produced more than they could possibly consume, and they invited the Indians to dinner, and voila, we got Thanksgiving, and that's what it was: inviting the Indians to dinner and giving thanks for all the plenty is the true story of Thanksgiving" (The Real Story of the First Thanksgiving).

Thus, the first seasons in America were, in effect, a great experiment on the difference between government manipulation of the markets (socialism) and free market enterprise (capitalism). Have we learned our lessons from history or are we doomed to repeat them?

HOW DOES GOVERNMENT DEBT PLAY
A FACTOR IN THE FREE ENTERPRISE SYSTEM?

"We shall all consider ourselves unauthorized to saddle posterity with our debts, and morally bound to pay them ourselves; and consequently within what may be deemed the period of a generation, or the life of the majority." —Thomas Jefferson

For one to fully understand the process by which regulations are imposed, one must look to the overall effectiveness of government-run entities. These various entities, do not seek to run on a *for-profit* motive, like that in the free enterprise system. Rather, these programs are run in quite the opposite direction, and are ever-increasing in the amount of debt they incur.

September 11th has had a history of not being a very good day for Americans. On September 11, 1789, the new President Washington, appointed Alexander Hamilton to be Secretary of the Treasury. Washington admittedly, was not educated in high finance and trusted Hamilton explicitly on the subject. This may have been President Washington's gravest mistake. Hamilton took advantage of this scenario and went to work. Consequently, our first national bank, a forerunner to the Federal Reserve in 1913, was created.   Most of the Founders, believed strongly that any *necessary* debt incurred by a people should be paid off, and not passed on to the next generation. Unfortunately, that sentiment was short-lived.

For decades, individuals have argued that the privatization of programs such as Social Security, Prisons, Education, and a host of others offer great incentive and true competition. Let us take each one briefly. The privatization of Social Security offers the opportunity for individuals to, (through interest earning and annuity types of accounts) provide for their own individual welfare after they reach an age, whereby they can no longer support themselves through employment. With Social Security going broke (and now operating much like a legalized Ponzi Scheme), this argument is becoming stronger.

With regard to prisons, the states and federal governments have had the responsibility of containment, and through various internal programs, rehabilitation of criminals. While this can be effective, the argument is that the free enterprise system and privatization of these institutions will provide opportunity for specific labor output that can result in increased production. Furthermore, privatization can cause a byproduct of prisoner skill-sets and training to be used when shorter-term inmates are released from their sentences. They are thus able to give something back to the community, and provide a better life for themselves. Some states are already benefiting from the privatization of prisons.

The privatization of education offers, the motivation of providing the best education possible. Educators are incentivized through a performance-based structure to advance their students through true learning. This occurs because schools with poor teachers and uninterested staff offer the student no real incentive. In turn, this will affect the decisions of the parents and children as to where they choose to participate in education. Where a crowded school is currently evidence of a lack of quality education, inefficiency, and wasteful spending, the exact opposite is true in the private sector. A crowded school (as with a crowded restaurant or marketplace) is evidence of the patronage or quality, and a sign that expansion may be necessary.

In each of the examples presented, the government, (as an entity who has taken the responsibility out of the hands of the people) has no true interest in refraining from excessive debt. Instead, they stand with their hands out hoarding whatever penny may fall from the coffers to their collection cup. Regulations imposed upon these programs are often not adhered to or followed since the government would have to hold itself accountable. Equally so, excessive debt, as adopted by governments, cannot fully be respected as a true concern. As governments are quick to offer any remedy as long as it does not relate to a more conservative spending approach. Taxes are levied upon the citizenry in the form of the IRS, the Federal Reserve printing money, and Congress borrowing from a foreign entity. These immoral actions are committed time after time to support the excessive spending that the government continues to perpetuate to keep such social programs in operation.

As taxes are increased to support government run entities, funding is shifted from one social program to another, the efficiency of the output is diminished, and communities are adversely affected. A group of individuals who pay into a Social Security system run by a government agency, stand to lose what he/she has worked a lifetime for, and the government bureaucracy over the program, is not incentivized to ensure those funds are managed properly. A private entity can provide more personal accountability to the individual for managing those funds. While the prison system is meant to incarcerate individuals who violate the laws of the land, it is only a private entity that can leverage the skill-set and labor generated by a continual workforce in a productive manner. If a system of education is made up of individuals who understand competition, this leads to an increased level of teaching, greater understanding, learning, and a stronger, more competitive generation by which all members of society can benefit from as a consequence. Should any of these private entities misrepresent or willfully mislead, the court system is in place to provide the equal protection of the law. Where does one turn when encountering inefficiencies within government run systems, the realization of taxes, along with regulations and fees imposed upon the citizenry to support the ever-mounting debt incurred by these inefficient programs? As with our current system, there is no true recourse against a government run agency, when the government run court system also protects that agency. The fox is truly guarding the hen-house.

GOLD AND SILVER

"No state shall make anything but gold and silver coin as tender in payments of debts."
      —*Article I, Section 10, clause 1 of the Constitution*

There is, an important place for government in the economy beyond the courts. For commerce to be efficient and fair, there is a need to regulate the form of exchange. For that form of currency to be viable, it should have intrinsic value, not be in great abundance, but portable, non-perishable, able to be easily divided into smaller parts, and be precisely measured. Precious metals (gold and silver) meet these requirements.

Though this country started with a reliance on such metals, we have fallen a long way since then. Our currency is no longer backed by gold, silver, or even tin. In 1971, Nixon saw to it that the government would no longer need to make sure their spending was backed by real, tangible assets. A true fiat currency ensued.

Fiat currencies have been tried before. The Weimar Republic, Zimbabwe, and the Colonies of America (during the Revolution) are examples. It did not work out well for them. It will not work out well in the end for us. The only way to stabilize our nation's economy is to get back to the Gold Standard and back to an honest financial system.

CONCLUSION

"I am for doing good to the poor, but I differ in opinion of the means. I think the best way of doing good to the poor, is not making them easy in poverty, but leading or driving them out of it. In my youth I travelled much, and I observed in different countries, that the more public provisions were made for the poor, the less they provided for themselves, and of course became poorer. And, on the contrary, the less was done for them, the more they did for themselves, and became richer." —Benjamin Franklin

As with any of our society's concerns, handling them at the most local and basic levels is efficient. This provides a level of accountability among the citizens of any given society to each other. By virtue of this accountability, the prosperity each individual seeks for him/herself can be greatly enhanced, achieved, and maintained through the free enterprise system. This necessitates the use and implementation of the mind to innovate for oneself along with respect for the rights of others. Those regulations imposed upon each industry are, by virtue of self-interest, self-imposed and the system of the courts set up to protect the rights of the individual, provides the necessary last resort.

It is this very system that limits the amount of debt taken on by governments and subsequently passes the savings on to its citizens. Without such system in place, governments continue to spend, debt continues to rise, taxes continue to be imposed, private property, and individual prosperity is greatly limited.

CHAPTER XIII

<hr>

The family, in its traditional form, as ordained by God, is the core unit of free society.

"There is certainly no country in the world where the tie of marriage is more respected than in America, or where conjugal happiness is more highly or worthily appreciated."—Alex de Tocqueville

INTRODUCTION

"The subjection of a minor places in the father a temporary government, which terminates with the minority of the child: and the honour due from a child, places in the parents a perpetual right to respect, reverence, support and compliance too, more or less, as the father's care, cost, and kindness in his education, has been more or less. This ends not with minority, but holds in all parts and conditions of a man's life... The nourishment and education of their children is a charge so incumbent on parents for their children's good, that nothing can absolve them from taking care of it." –John Locke

What does a principle related to the family have to do with a book about the government? In a word, everything. Governments will not survive if the family unit is ever changing and drifting from its traditional form. If governing powers within a unit (parents) are limited as to strip and shift all responsibility and accountability to the State, society as a whole, is in danger of destruction. Strong words indeed. However, the family is at the very nucleolus of all governing institutions. The family unit is a governing body itself, made up of individual citizens. Rules and laws are set in place for the benefit of its members, the protection of each member's rights, and for the advancement of the family unit as a whole. This family unit is divine in its origins. It should first be looked at as an example of how to govern. If functioning properly, its members learn, grow, and thrive in an environment meant to protect and foster such movement.

The examples seen in families across the country show the differences between those family units that live by, and adhere to principles and those who govern strictly by emotion. This contrast provides ample evidence for the manner in which one could govern a community, large or small. These communities, if based upon and founded in the very same principles relating to family governance, will thrive and ever increase. If these communities, states, and countries base their decisions, programs, and governance upon emotional whims difficulty, poverty, and eventual slavery to some intangible master will inevitably be the end result. The principle-based family must not only be upheld and safeguarded, it must be applauded as a specimen and pattern fit for all governments.

THE FAMILY UNIT

"It is in the love of one's family only that heartfelt happiness is known. By a law of our nature, we cannot be happy without the endearing connections of a family."—Thomas Jefferson

A family, as a rule, must always be more than one individual. Surely, how can there be a son without first their being a father and mother? A man and woman become a new family unit when they join together in matrimony. Otherwise, each individual is first and only a member of a separate family unit. Once a man and women enter into this new life together, the two of them become (though still bound to mother and father) their own, distinct family.

This family unit is responsible to itself for the care and management of its members. Decisions made are fiscal, social, medical, spiritual, physical, emotional, educational, etc. At times, multiple types of employment are necessary to meet the needs of each member. As this family grows in number, additional conversations may be had regarding its changing nature. Decisions are undertaken, usually by both parents (with input at times from the children), and the family proceeds in unity with any given situation. When difficulty within the family unit exceeds the member's ability to handle and overcome, extended families can function as a support system.

Families range in size and structure, but operate as an individual unit in order to move forward with effectiveness. If one parent takes on the responsibility of managing family finances and the other needlessly spends without proper communication, frustration will surely follow. This puts the family unit nearly at a standstill, until family finances can again be managed effectively. As with any other area of management within the family unit, communication must be maintained to function properly.

This unit is the most basic form of governance outside of personal self-governance. Parents serve as governmental bodies, similar in nature to a legislature and executive combined. They serve to determine the rules and laws that are necessary for the benefit of every member within the family. Once these rules and laws are in place, systems set up to enforce them and are devised. When a family member violates a rule or law, much like in society today, punishments set are imposed upon the violator. Thus, the parents also function as a loving yet solid judiciary branch.

As the family progresses in size, additional members (citizens) enter into the family. Supplementary rules or laws are then set in order to accommodate the changing family unit as members enter in or find themselves at the appropriate time, leaving and starting their own family units. Throughout this process, parents are entrusted with the care and nurture of their children, and they provide opportunities to learn self-reliance and discover how to function and run their own family. Thus, the cycle continues.

THE TRADITIONALLY HELD VIEW OF THE FAMILY

"I know of no Medicine fit to diminish the violent natural Inclinations you mention; and if I did, I think I should not communicate it to you. Marriage is the proper Remedy. It is the most natural State of Man, and therefore the State in which you are most likely to find solid Happiness...It is the Man and Woman united that make the complete human Being." —Benjamin Franklin

Traditionally, the view of a family has been a husband and a wife (and may also include children). In recent time, however, the view of family has shifted to that which may or may not include both the husband and wife. This view of the family changes to accommodate families that have been altered through divorce, death, or some other circumstance. Nevertheless, the family unit, in its traditional form, always first begins with a man and woman entering into the bonds of matrimony.

Same gender groups, advocating for the right to marry, argue that a family can be one, with two fathers, two mothers, or any other concoction that can be imagined. *What matters is that they love one another*, is concluded frequently through the media. Quotes, statistics, and *facts* are made to favor their position. They scream for *equal rights* and condemn what they see as *discrimination* against their desires. The problem is this; what they want, *equal treatment under the law*, is unrelated to what they are crying for, *marriage*. What is at play is nothing more than euphemisms. As is the case with most words, the definition of marriage has changed over time. Noah Webster was a contemporary of the Founders. In his 1828 Dictionary, the definition of marriage is as follows, "The act of uniting a man and woman for life; wedlock; the legal union of a man and woman for life. Marriage is a contract both civil and religious, by which the parties engage to live together in mutual affection and fidelity; till death shall separate them. Marriage was instituted by God himself for the purpose of preventing the promiscuous intercourse of the sexes, for promoting domestic felicity, and for securing the maintenance and education of children." In the 21st Century, the definition of marriage, as found in the 2010 Merriam-Webster Online Dictionary is "the state of being united to a person of the opposite sex as husband or wife in a consensual and contractual relationship recognized by law; the state of being united to a person of the same sex in a relationship like that of a traditional marriage <same-sex marriage>; the mutual relation of married persons; the institution whereby individuals are joined in a marriage; an act of marrying or the rite by which the married status is effected; especially: the wedding ceremony and attendant festivities or formalities; an intimate or close union." Same word; very different meanings. The majority of those crying foul over the definition of marriage are not so much in favor of *being married* as they are positioning themselves to be treated equally under the law. To this, I say *grant them their wish*. In fact, the law should treat them equally. The definition of the word *marriage*, however, should be left as it was intended in the beginning. When Adam and Eve were joined together, it was not the State who issued the marriage certificate. It was not the State who said that their marriage now entitled them to file their IRS 1040 *filing jointly*. It was not the State which handled tax credits, health coverage, community property, or welfare checks differently due to their marital status. If we are going to have a discussion about the definition of marriage, let's have a discussion about where the State has a stake in the institution.

Marriage was intended in the beginning to be a contract entered into and involving three different parties. Those parties were man, woman, and the Lord. Those who scream for the *separation of church and state* often forget it was the State who imposed on the God-given institution of marriage to begin with. Maybe there ought to be some separation there. This contract is between a man and a woman, since it is only a man and woman that can reproduce and create new life without the involvement of science to alter the natural reproductive process.

While consenting adults are free to choose the relationships, they enter into as a matter of principle, a proposed marriage between of anything other than one between a man to a woman, is anything but traditional and cannot be considered the same. Only in the traditional family can one find the proper pattern for governance. It is made up of a set of adults that can become natural parents whose entire focus from then on is designed to provide, teach, train, and assist in the creation of an increasing family unit. While these are not exclusive to a husband and wife relationship and could likewise be accomplished by a same gender couple, the power to procreate cannot be found in anything other than the traditional male and female relationship.

ORDAINED BY GOD

"Therefore shall a man leave his father and his mother, and shall cleave unto his wife: and they shall be one flesh."
—KJV Genesis 2:24

As God is the ultimate in authority on all things, it is His sanction that should be considered paramount. Acknowledgement of the Divine, and His role within the bonds of matrimony, is something that should be considered for any marriage to succeed. Personalities are constantly changing and evolving with each successive experience. Many important moments in the life of a couple are greatly tested with challenges and difficulty. These challenges are temporal in nature and can cover a broad spectrum of issues ranging from financial stresses to extended family relations. Marital strife can stem from emotional or physical difficulties, as well as the lack of education.

Great care and responsibility falls upon a man and woman when they choose to enter into such a bond. A marriage is a contract and partnership with each other, and if this new couple wishes the greatest opportunity for success, they must include the Creator. This contract is such that a man promises to perform certain duties within his role. Likewise, the woman in her role makes equal commitments. This is not a 50-50 split in responsibility and companionship making up the full 100%, but rather one of 100% devotion and commitment to each other. As it relates to God and the contract this couple enters into, it must likewise be a 100% devotion to God.

Man and woman, as commanded in the beginning, are meant to procreate and bring forth much fruit. The child is brought into the world and experiences its own greatest opportunity for success if this new life is formed under the contract of matrimony. While success can be achieved in single parent households, there can be no replacement for the husband and wife working together to teach and mold the life of a child into a productive, self-reliant member of society. It is also possible, and much evidence would concur, that children in same-sex partnership households can also achieve success in raising a child to be an outstanding and contributing member of society. However, as it relates marriage, we must first examine what some may refer to as the first law as outlined in the first Book of Genesis. It was God that stated, "Be fruitful, and multiply, and replenish the earth..." (*KJV* Genesis 1:28). As evidence from this passage of scripture, we note that only man and woman have the ability to create new human life. This is how the pattern was to be set in the beginning, and God is not interested in political correctness. Creating man and woman, then commanding them to multiply, designates the purpose, and the differences between the two sexes. How they are to operate, and that it was indeed divinely inspired, is also set forth.

Biblical law teaches that "Neither is the man without the woman, neither the woman without the man, in the Lord" (*KJV* 1 Corinthians 11:11). Here, the apostle Paul teaches that man and woman are to become husband and wife, inseparable and working together as a single unit, together with the Lord. This is the natural order of things. Further, we learn through ancient scripture that those within the family unit, namely the children, are to *honor* both father and mother together, equally. This is a pattern for governance. We see an immediate recognition of the responsibility to govern as a unit; the recognition that this governing is to be done in conjunction with the Lord, and a mutual respect for those who are called to lead the family.

CORE UNIT OF A FREE SOCIETY

"Marriage, or a union of the sexes, though it be in itself on of the smallest societies, is the original fountain from whence the greatest and most extensive governments have derived their beings."
—*Benjamin Franklin*

It is fitting to question from time to time where one currently fits, in any given relationship. By this knowledge, one may discover and develop in those areas which will create the most value for the members of the relationship and ultimately strengthen it. This small unit of individuals we call family is, in one sense, a mini representation of a city, county, state, or federal government. Any large Lego™ city must first start with individual blocks of red, yellow, green, or blue. Upon these smaller units, the whole is formed.

Though parents are not *elected* by their children to rule, they are responsible to them to lead in a fashion that is *representative* of their best interest. How these and all families govern themselves, largely determines how they will govern as a whole. If a family governs purely upon the emotions of its members without specific plans and founding principles, then the family is subject to the outside influences that can neither be fully anticipated nor controlled. Likewise, school districts, city councils, county commissions, state legislators, and federal law-makers are simply moms, dads, and individuals trying as best they can, to govern. That governance like all things begins at home.

Communities made up of several, independent family units are bound by their own set of rules and laws. Freedom exists within a society or community, where the individual or family has the ability to decide on their own what they will or will not do. Provided no laws pertaining to the rights of others are broken, members of any society can only count themselves truly free, when this occurs. When a husband and wife are told how they must operate in the rearing of their children, *for the good of society*, freedom is hindered. When government bodies impose laws and regulation as to that which parents are to teach their children, freedom is again, hindered.

Should all families be determined to govern themselves based upon principles, the ability to see when elected officials have over-reached their authority, would be magnified. One could easily point out where local, state, and federal governments have violated such principles by applying them to how the family is governed. Every issue, program, or proposed legislation could then be brought down to the most basic and core unit, the family. For example, if a family found themselves swallowed in consumer debt, would it make sense to *spend their way out of it*? Why is the principle any different when the Speaker of the House proposes the same tactic for a nation? Would it be right for a mother to take one of Johnny's two teddy bears and give it to Suzy to *help spread the wealth around*? Why then, do we accept such rhetoric from our President? Such proposals could be weighed as to how it would affect the family by likening it to this smallest form of government. This keeps a free society free. A society will not thrive if its proposed laws and regulations harm the family unit.

CONCLUSION

> *"As long as Property exists, it will accumulate in Individuals and Families. As long as Marriage exists, Knowledge, Property and Influence will accumulate in Families."* —John Adams

Principles govern, it is those families who adhere to principles that are in the greatest position to not only govern themselves successfully, but to also become a positive influence within their communities. Such a family unit functions in a manner irrespective of circumstance and social standing as it relates to wealth, national origin, and or health. Their ability to determine the most productive course, assists in holding those elected to govern equally within their community. This sort of family fosters generational progress as it passes onto each successive generation the truths and moral code by which to live and produce. Financial success and stability is weighed by principle. Interaction with others is weighed by principle. Any and all decisions made by a family, or proposed to such a family, is always weighed first, by principle.

The traditional emblem as it relates to the family is one ordained, and sanctioned by God. Such a designation is that of man, woman, and where applicable, child. Such a family infringes upon no one and as a matter of principle, such a family will shift their burdens upon no one. As they recognize their Creator, understand the importance of becoming productive members of society, and seek to alleviate any difficulty, others within their community may encounter. They then become part of the solution rather than part of the problem. This substance of which they will first provide is not the substance of material wealth, but rather the substance of their knowledge concerning living by principles. Seeking to strengthen those around them through education, experience, and a willingness to continually learn and improve themselves, is the key to changing the difficulties we currently find our nation in. Undeniably, this family unit, found in its traditional form as it is ordained by God, is the very core unit that makes up a free and liberated society.

CHAPTER XIV

※·⁘·※

How it all fits together

"We do not need more material development, we need more spiritual development. We do not need more intellectual power, we need more moral power. We do not need more knowledge, we need more character. We do not need more government, we need more culture. We do not need more law, we need more religion...It is that side which is the foundation of all else. If the foundation be firm, the superstructure will stand." —Calvin Coolidge

INTRODUCTION

"We must forge ahead always! Knowledge of the enemy helps develop the wisdom and discernment which are essential if we are to deal with him effectively. ...The individual who assumes a cloak of neutrality in the present struggle is neither intellectual nor liberal. He cannot be religious. He is not neutral. At best, he is the dupe of forces which are wholly evil." —J. Edgar Hoover

The 12 Principles of Liberty™ are just that, the very principles mankind must follow, and live by if they are to restore and maintain their freedoms. No one individual can do it alone. It will take a group of people to recognize the truths they contain and hold those whom they elect, accountable. Apathy must not win out to ignorance; for an ignorant man can be taught, but an apathetic man will simply lack the interest to even try. The moral code of values we subscribe to will either preserve freedom or destroy it. We are the stewards, and this is our choice.

These principles build upon one another, and construct the moral code of values by which any productive family, community, or country is to live under to remain free and prosperous. In order to live free, we must recognize and live the following truths: 1) God is the creator and source of those rights we have for so long taken for granted. 2) Man cannot strip from other men those rights he never held the authority over in the first place. 3) The governments of the world are to be set up as a protector of these rights; not a destroyer of them. 4) Man can alter the organization by which he is governed. 5) Man is justified in the eyes of his Creator in defending his natural rights. 6) Only a moral and educated people can create the laws meant to protect the rights enjoyed by all men. 7) Only through proper representation can every voice be heard. 8) A governing body must be maintained at a local and *touchable* level to ensure accountability. 9) All are equal in the eyes of God, the law and in the manner in which their rights are to be protected. 10) Every man can choose but must accept the ultimate responsibility for his choices. 11) In order for prosperity to occur for anyone, the fruits of labor must remain his or her own; not taken and distributed among the idle among us, and 12) The family unit, in its original and traditional form, is inspired of God and must be held inviolate for a society to remain free. To deny these truths is to deny one's own existence, thus, making the deceiver the deceived.

These truths are concrete. They must be the *true north* in the lives of any man or woman who seeks to hold political office; every man and woman who seeks to unite through matrimony and become parents, who willingly rear and raise their children; and for the life of any child who seeks to become a productive individual in society. What life becomes for each of us is what we choose individually, and what it becomes for future generations will largely depend on the moral code we adopt for ourselves. Those of the younger generation are watching, and they are indeed learning. Hence, the question becomes, *what is it we are teaching them?*

A MOST DESTRUCTIVE GAME

> *"Single acts of tyranny many be ascribed to the accidental opinion of a day; but a series of oppressions, begun at a distinguished period, and pursued unalterably through every change of ministers, too plainly prove a deliberate, systematical plan of reducing us to Slavery." —Thomas Jefferson*

Not more than a year ago I watched, as a group of children played a very telling game. This game they played, was one they had just invented on their own, a short time prior to me observing their fun. As I watched and listened intently, I began to learn something about these children. I discovered something about the mindsets and perspectives they had commenced to adopt at a very early age. While playing their game, I noted that no arguing or complaining was heard from any of the children. There was no commenting on how others were cheating, or not playing fairly. Each child played their individual roles within the game as though they came natural. This all seemed innocent enough until I discovered the small details of this most destructive game they were playing. One very concerning thing about this game was that it was created by children, yet it mirrored so closely the world in which some live. The more I contemplated it, the more it made sense to me. The fact that these young children came up with the game on their own was not uncommon, after all. Children will often draw from experiences and the world around them in their make believe playing. What was most startling, however, was the game's objective. Though it was simply children playing that I was observing, the nature of the game was quite telling.

'Soldiers and Slaves' was the name of this game, and there was no way to win. *Like the song that never ends*, you just kept on playing.

Before the game commenced, the group of children determined which among them would be the Soldiers' and which among them would be the Slaves'. The children outlined at the very onset, which group would be the responsible party during game. The Soldiers' were to be in charge of the Slaves' and the Slaves' simply did what was commanded of them, no questions asked. One would think that the choice to be a Slave is one that no child would willingly decide. Sure enough, some were disposed to play the role. Opportunities were given throughout the game for Slaves' to be promoted to a Soldier. This helped in understanding why one might relent to beginning the game as a Slave. Equally so, a Soldier could under certain circumstances, be demoted to a Slave. The primary purpose of the game, however, was for the Soldiers' to make the lives of the Slaves' *as horrible* as possible. The roles were assigned and the game began.

During the playing of what was referred to by the oldest of the children as, 'The Game of Our Future,' I witnessed these Soldiers' spouting off ridiculously silly commands. One Slave was told to crawl back and forth until they were instructed to stop. Another was commanded to carry various toys from one area in which they were playing to another. They then had to carry them back again just a short time later. Nothing was commanded that was to be considered malicious, rather, their dictates were more counterproductive. As the game progressed, the Soldiers began being more direct with their commands and would often shoot foam bullets from toy guns in the direction of the Slaves' if they noticed the Slaves' talking to one another. At one point, a Soldier suggested that the Slaves' should pay a fine for disobeying an order. Thereafter, they began spouting off a pretended sum of money to be paid whenever their *leaderly* instincts dictated it.

At times, the Soldiers' would select one from the crowd of Slaves' and make them their personal assistant for a time. The work of the assistant Slave was simple; give the commands and punishments in place of the master Soldier so that he or she could rest and enjoy some free time. Punishments would be imposed for not fulfilling a command quickly and could range from giving the Soldier a ride on the Slave's back to being shunned and ignored by the others. Community service was common in the group of Slaves'. However, it was always meant to benefit the community of Soldiers', never the Slaves.'

When a Slave was obedient and the Soldiers' felt that the Slave might make a good Soldier, there was a promotion. This promotion meant the Slave, although a newly promoted Soldier, could be with the rest of the Soldiers'. They could give commands, hand out punishments for non-compliance, and even impose upon other Slaves' in whatever manner they chose. While each Slave throughout the game worked

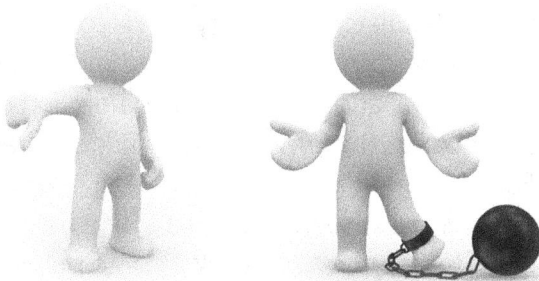

to become a Soldier, a Guard-Soldier was in constant observation of his or her fellow Soldiers'. The purpose of this guard was to see if any fellow Soldier warranted a demotion to a Slave. Demotions would happen if one Soldier caught another Soldier taking any degree of compassion on a Slave or feeling that a Slave's punishment was too harsh. Immediately, the tender Soldier becomes a Slave. Their punishment for empathy was to see what life was like from the *other side*.

The game would then continue, with no final objective. No one person would stand out and claim victory. The Slaves' wanted to become the Soldiers' and the Soldiers' were watching each other to avoid becoming the Slaves'. It was a vicious cycle. The entire purpose was to create an environment where a group of people would constantly be Slaves' to a group of Soldiers', and to convince them to be such willingly. Never to win. Never to progress. Always the same.

After several hours of play, the children finally became tired of their little game. I had observed for some time and ventured to ask the oldest why 'Soldiers and Slaves?' Her response was quick, immediate, and full of real life examples. She quipped, "Well, if you want to get all *governmenty* about it, the Soldiers' are the Dictators and the Slaves' are the Citizens."

And there I sat, having watched 'The Game of Our Future.' Here were mere children, yet they understood perfectly the *role of a Dictator*. They knew a tyrant's sole mission was to make life for the citizen *horrible* with counterproductive activities, great burdens and to laden them with *heavy taxes*. They somehow comprehended the role of the Soldier as seeking to find loyal subjects to promote, and help them inflict punishment upon their fellow citizens in behalf of their master Soldier. These *great* Soldiers', who every Slave sought to become, would constantly be watching their own backs, knowing one of their own would betray them, and could quickly be demoted to a Slave. I watched these children, these young, innocent children, play 'The Game of Our Future.'

As ominous as this game sounds, and the concern this would bring to any true lover of freedom, all is not lost. Prior to publication of this book, the details of this, 'The Game of Our Future' were examined with the inventor. Discussions with the oldest of these children were had, as an attempt to gain clarity and be certain that the facts of the game presented were indeed accurate and fairly represented. During this discussion the child asked, "What are you going to be doing with the information on the game?" The child was informed that the message of the game, and what it taught were valuable examples of what life becomes when citizens of any nation abandon principle. Further, it was explained that this very book, *Restoring America*, was a *declaration of principles* that would be written and in the concluding chapter the details and story of this game would be presented. Happily, I heard the following response, "Wait, you did not ask my permission to include a game that I invented. You will have to pay me for the use in your book first." With that, I smiled, this child truly understood, and wanted to live by the Free Enterprise System.

It is the very system of Capitalism through innovation within the freedom of Free Enterprise, that *what one created, one owned*. This helped our country become the greatest nation on the face of the earth. Weather or not this child lives under a system of freedom we once enjoyed, or under the tyrannical rule of the game she chose to play, will be largely determined by each of us in the present day.

MUCH WORK LEFT TO DO

"Today, as never before, America has need for men and women who possess the moral strength and courage of our forefathers—modern day patriots, with pride in our country and faith in freedom, unafraid to declare to anyone in the world, 'I believe in liberty. I believe in justice. I will fight, if need be, to defend the dignity of man." —J. Edgar Hoover

There should be no doubt that our work is cut out for each of us regarding the preservation of our freedom. We must continually fight for that which is worth fighting for. The liberties we enjoy will not be protected simply because we *hope* for it. No amount of hope will restore this country to the level of greatness it once held in the eyes of the world, nor will clever bromides, allow this country to overcome and become greater still. A call to action is a rallying cry for those who are not moved otherwise. There are those who would sit idle until a clear course is cut before them. But who among you will first blaze and cut the path for others to see? I have heard it said many times, that men and women of greatness are heroes to the world because in the midst of the darkness, they lead all towards the light of day. I say, this is not so. Instead, the men and women, the heroes of the world, are such because in the midst of darkness, they are *themselves*, the light.

We have plenty of work left to perform; many people within our circles of influence to educate, inform, and lock arms within this battle for freedom. What we do now will affect not only the lives of our children, but also that of our children's children. They look to us as the guardians of their freedom, and at least for this moment in our history, we are the stewards of their liberty. Abraham Lincoln once said, "The world will little note, nor long remember what we say here." What we say is of little consequence when compared to that which we do. It is time to do!

Individuals of character and integrity are forged through consistent and measurable actions that are rooted in principle, and not purely upon emotions. By becoming such an individual, one develops the ability to self-govern and determine their own destiny. If men and women are to be found without such character and integrity, then those whom they have chosen to lead them, will do so at their own peril. Character determines the strength of a nation, integrity holds the nation to its course, and principles provide the method to build the very strength needed for every nation that expects to be free.

HOW WE SAVE OUR COUNTRY, COMMUNITY, AND FAMILIES

"It is substantially true, that virtue or morality is a necessary spring of popular government." —George Washington

Living a life of principle, and holding ourselves accountable to the principles which we advocate, is the very first step in restoring what we have lost, and preserving that which we still have. This is not a part-time, weekend-only endeavor. We must meet together often to learn and teach one another how to identify principles lived or violated in the world around us. If violations are found, we must seek to correct them based upon principle, to ensure the rights of all man and women are protected. As we meet together, we must determine what we can most affect at the local level. A family preserves and protects itself as a family. A community works to preserve and protect itself as the community. A country, preserves and protects itself as a country, based on principles.

Within the *United in Liberty* group, Community Action Committees (CACs) are made up of members consisting of several families in each community. These members work together to hold the local leaders of their community accountable to living by principle. They weigh each decision being made in City Councils, Home Owners Associations, Parent Teacher Organizations, School Boards, County Government Meetings,, and in any other entity where a voice is represented by someone other than their own. Communities are held accountable to the members within. Thus, each community can govern itself and its decisions based on principle. Together, they right those wrongs, or restore those freedoms, which have been infringed upon, one at a time. This translates to the very mission of *United in Liberty*, "**Saving the Constitution, One Community at a Time.**" This is a daunting task if taken in totality. Rather, let's review the mission piece by piece.

First, to the topic of **Saving the Constitution**. This may be a monumental expectation, but the preservation of our original, representative form of government is essential if the rights of every man are to be protected. It cannot be saved in part. All rights vouchsafed, therein build upon one another. If we are going to be successful, we must work to save it all.

Second, doing it **One Community at a Time**. It is really a fallacy to believe that there is anything such as *group think*. Each family, group, community, tribe, state, or country is only a sum of its parts, the individual. If we start with the individual who takes accountability within his or her own family, we begin with man's mind. All men can, and do, think independent of one another. If we can educate just one, we can affect the whole. The individual works to educate his or her own family. The family works with other families to check and balance their own community, based upon principle. There is no other way. For a community in California to legislate how a community in Montana should govern makes no logical sense. Likewise, a group of elected officials in our Nation's Capitol have no true understanding of what take place at a local level. Why we have left the governing of our entire country to one small corner is something to be considered. We do not advocate for, nor are we promoting an abandonment of our Federal Government. On the contrary, we simply wish it to be returned to its original intent. This will only happen when communities across the country assume control for themselves. Such local accountability allows for communities within their particular states to hold state representatives accountable for good, principled-based government. This will, as a matter of order, create the environment where elected representatives in each State represent their constituents in a principle-based manner while they serve in Washington. If an individual is out of step, or violating *The 12 Principles of Liberty*™, they should be removed from office and replaced, regardless of what *special interest* is working to keep them there.

The 12 Principles of Liberty™ are not exclusive to government as it relates to communities, states, or countries. Rather, the principles can be applied all the way down to the most basic unit—the family. This is where good men and women are raised. This is where we find our elected officials; those we call on to represent our voices. We must live such principles in our own lives and families. As we do, we ensure that those we call upon are just, and remain just. We will then understand how they will govern in any given circumstance, for their code will be our own. A refusal by any elected official to live by principle will have unintended consequences. The result we achieve is based upon this supreme choice. It is real. It is the only way, short of a costly revolution, that our freedoms can be restored.

May we be certain in our choices, deliberate in our applications, and willing to accept full responsibility for each. The alternative is akin to finding ourselves much like those who were in fear for their own security, notwithstanding the true lack of freedom they themselves created, listening to the character John Galt in the novel *Atlas Shrugged* by Ayn Rand. Speaking over the airwaves to the citizens of the country that adopted the wrong moral code said, "You have destroyed all that which you held to be evil and achieved all that which you held to be good. Why, then, do you shrink in horror from the sight of the world around you? That world is not the product of your sins, it is the product and the image of your virtues. It is your moral ideal brought into reality in its full and final perfection."

CONCLUSION

"You and I have a rendezvous with destiny. We will preserve for our children this, the last best hope of man on earth, or we will sentence them to take the first step into a thousand years of darkness. If we fail, at least let our children and our children's children

say of us we justified our brief moment here. We did all that could be done." —Ronald Reagan

We invite you to consider what it is we seek to accomplish. If the cause is just, we further extend the invitation for you to join us in this mission. People, not one man or one woman—but united together in force, best preserve freedom for people. Join with us, associate with us as well as with others who are about the very same mission of which we speak. Not any one organization will be able to right the course of which we have drifted from far too long. There will be those that are entirely about the education necessary to govern. We applaud and support those organizations for their work and efforts. They will be of tremendous value. There will be groups and associations who believe that a grassroots, mobile course of action, with *boots on the ground*, is the focus that should be pursued. These are they who knock on doors and speak one-on-one with members of the community to educate and seek, to awaken them from the sleep that apathy brings upon them. Still, others will protest those who would trample the rights of men and women. To such groups, we give our thanks and lend our support. To stand together, and boldly reveal that which destroyers of freedom wish to remain hidden, takes great courage and patriotism. There are untold ways that we can and must work together, to preserve and restore our liberties.

Freedom is not free and liberty is lost to the man who seeks to be completely secured. Maximum security is anything but. Join with us today. We need your voice and your assistance. Bring others with you. A line has been drawn in the sand. A choice must be made. We are about a difficult work and one which we can only accomplish together. On which side of the line do you stand in this cause of freedom and liberty? Make the choice in the battle for freedom to help in "***Saving the Constitution, One Community at a Time.***"

CHAPTER XV

Taking individual action

"You must be the change you wish to see in the world.
— Mohandas Karamchand Gandhi

As you have read, you may have felt moved to do more than just gain knowledge. We hope you have gained or fostered a desire to get involved in the fight for freedom, and we invite you to act on your convictions. There are many groups on a local and national level that you can begin to *do something*. There are many action items that you can do individually and begin today. What you do, does not have to involve *United in Liberty*.

Whatever you do, please do not put down this book, think it was a nice read, and not have it cause you to change anything in your life. The fact is, if you do not commit to do something different today while the emotions are high, you will likely not do anything different at all. Thus, your time spent reading this book will be wasted. If, what you have read causes you to do even one, minor thing for the cause for freedom, it has been a success.

For those who wish for a better world and want to be involved in meaningful ways, we offer these following options:

BECOME A MEMBER OF UNITED IN LIBERTY

Visit www.unitedinliberty.org to learn more about our mission and our vision. This will assist you in understanding the purpose of this publication.

United in Liberty is doing more than just talking about the principles of freedom. We are actively working to protect every American's freedom by advocating for principle-based solutions to the challenges we face. To benefit from *United in Liberty*, you should first become a Member, and then join a local Community Action Committee™ (CAC). The purpose of *United in Liberty* is not to grow the organization into one large society with as many members as possible, but rather, build small community groups that meet frequently together in member's homes.

There is no financial commitment to become a member of *United in Liberty*, the only commitment we ask of you is that you give your time. With the many challenges we face as a nation and in our own individual communities, it is clear that there is a great need for good, sound, principally-minded individuals that can help lead our communities in the direction our Founding Fathers had originally envisioned.

For those of you that would like to join *United in Liberty* please go to our website and fill out our membership application. This is the first step. You should then join a local CAC or start one of your own. The CAC meetings are where the real work gets accomplished.

The CAC has a Community Action Leader, two Assistants, a Record Keeper, and Members. They meet frequently for two hours. During that meeting, both education and action happens. The first portion of the meeting is a colloquium discussion about a chapter of *Restoring America: 12 Principles that will Save our Country, Communities, and Families* or something from our library consisting of a classic, principle-based book that the group is currently reading. The second hour is spent discussing local issues, and what will be done to affect them. This part of the meeting is dedicated to discussion of what is going on in the local community. The issues affecting *The 12 Principles of Liberty*™ are focused on, and discussed. If principles are being violated within the community, members of *United in Liberty* are acting to solve that problem. As a group, they decide what is happening, how best to respond, and assignments are made. Proactive events such as petitioning, educating neighbors, writing to Congressmen, letters to the editor, engaging in meaningful conversations, attending and speaking out in local City Council, and school board meetings, etc. are the backbone of the CAC.

If you are interested in becoming part of the solution, we invite you to visit our website and become a member today. Take the first step in "***Saving the Constitution, One Community at a Time.***"

AFFILIATE WITH UNITED IN LIBERTY

You do not need to be a member of *United in Liberty* to enjoy its benefits. One of the great geniuses of *United in Liberty* is that, rather than take you from the group you already belong to, we seek to unify all patriotic groups through endorsements. An endorsement is like a "Better Business Bureau of Patriotism." We believe the cause of freedom can best move forward if all groups who love liberty seek to be united in communication and political activism. Whether you are an individual or a member of a larger, like-minded organization, we invite you to join us in the fight to restore our Nation to the ideals it was founded upon.

A Representative Republic is organized in such a way that people, can work together to change the system for the better. Maybe you have been frustrated as a group when you try to change legislation, policy, laws, etc. and the numbers are just not there to do so. One of the benefits of *United in Liberty* is that we can work together for change because there is strength in numbers and united by principle.

Though your particular group may have its particular values and projects, we hope you will be willing to lend your support to the mission of *United in Liberty*. When a policy, politician, law, proposal, etc. seeks to threaten our liberties, we hope you (and your group) will unite with us in working together to prevent these abuses. In turn, when a policy, politician, law, proposal, etc. seeks to threaten your group's particular issue, we will be there (as a group) to stand with you. If you already belong to one of these groups, we hope you will associate with *United in Liberty* so that we might all work together in moving the cause of freedom. If you already belong to a freedom-loving group and want to affiliate with *United in Liberty*, we invite you to go to our website and contact us.

UNITED IN LIBERTY RADIO

Each week, the Co-founders of *United in Liberty*, Dustin Harris and Joe Olivas, are bringing you the most contemporary topics and relating them to *The 12 Principles of Liberty™*. *United in Liberty* Radio can be downloaded and heard each week on our website at no cost. There, you can also download and listen to past episodes as well.

These men are not your typical talk-radio hosts. Rather than simply offering up rhetoric and complaints regarding the news stories of the day, they break them down, apply them to principle, and give you action item suggestions. They are not about complaining, they are about identifying the principles that will lead to real solutions.

In a world full of negativity and principle violation, join the authors of *Restoring America: 12 Principles that will Save our Country, Communities, and Families* each week to get an uplift and a reminder of how principles work and what we should be doing to promote them.

AUDIO CDS

Looking for a specific topic? Want to know even more about *The 12 Principles of Liberty™*, how *United in Liberty* works, or what we can do to get back to the ideals espoused by the Founding Fathers? Audio CDs are available on our website at the online store. Both in-studio and live events are available for purchase.

These audio programs can be listened to over and over, and are a great way to stay reminded of the same principles learned in this book. They also make great gifts and are a wonderful way to introduce your family or friends to *United in Liberty*.

LIBRARY

Don't let your education begin and end here. These universal principles are found in many great publications. A large number of them are found in our online Library. Visit our website now to find out which ones you have read, need to brush up on, or read for the first time. Most of these books can also be purchased through our online store.

E-NEWSLETTERS

Enjoy the book? *United in Liberty* articles can frequently be found right in your email inbox. The *United in Liberty* E-newsletter is an electronic periodical, which breaks down current events and further delves into principles. If you would like to begin receiving the E-newsletter, go to our website and sign up today.

Want to participate? We love reading articles from supporters of *United in Liberty* and often publish them to a large audience through the E-newsletter. Email us your articles. You could be the next one to get published!

LECTURE SERIES

The *United in Liberty* Lecture Series is a great, low-cost way, to give a large group of patriots a powerful experience they will not soon forget. There is nothing quite as inspiring as a live-lecture! Both Dustin Harris and Joe Olivas are available to come to your home-town to speak directly about *The 12 Principles of Liberty™*, and how they relate to every level of government. Experience dynamic, engaging speakers that will uplift and motivate your attendees. For details, email them through the website.

OTHER PUBLICATIONS

Look for other publications by *United in Liberty* and the authors, Dustin Harris and Joe Olivas, yet to come.

These are in no way exclusive and all-encompassing. Whether you choose to be involved in *United in Liberty* or in other ways, we hope you will choose to be engaged in the restoration of our freedoms. If we do not start today, regardless of our busy calendars, it will be too late. In 1941, President Roosevelt gave to Winston Churchill a copy of the following poem by Henry Wadsworth Longfellow. Speaking to Churchill, Roosevelt said, "This verse applies to you people as well as to us."

O Ship of State
Thou, too, sail on, O Ship of State!
Sail on, O Union, strong and great!
Humanity with all its fears,
With all the hopes of future years,
Is hanging breathless on thy fate!

The ship of state is our great nation. We are at the helm. What we do in this nation not only affects our country, but all of humanity as they watch to see what we, the leaders of the world, will do next. The principles we live are applicable to our country, communities, families, and even to us as individuals. What does our future hold? It is time to turn this ship around as individuals and collectively as a nation, and sail back to the free and open waters of liberty!

ABOUT THE AUTHORS

DUSTIN HARRIS

Dustin was born and raised in Southeast Idaho. He was brought up in a political environment and taught by goodly parents to not take anything at face-value. Needless to say, sparks could fly around the Harris family dinner table.

Like many, he is concerned about the direction this Country is heading, and is bound and determined to do more than just complain from the sidelines. He is a strong believer in God and heavily involved in his faith.

Dustin has a Bachelor's Degree from Idaho State University in Corporate Training and Vocational Teacher Education, and a Masters Degree in Adult and Organizational Learning from the University of Idaho. His greatest education, however, has been self-induced.

He is an avid reader of history, government, self-improvement, business, and spiritual works. He is an entrepreneur and owns/operates multiple, small businesses. He loves the outdoors. He and his wife, Kami, have four children.

JOE OLIVAS

Originally from Los Angeles, CA, Joe was fortunate to meet and fall in love with a wonderful woman, and together they have three amazing children who are a very big part of their lives. Over the last several years, he and his wife Laura have become even more deliberate about teaching their young children who they are, who they can become, and who God knows them to be. This is no small thing, as every individual is faced with many challenges from day-to-day, and constantly fight against that which we each know to be true. However, they equally understand that it is in how they choose to view these challenges, that makes all of the difference in the world, for themselves and their children.

Joe firmly believes that productive goals and ambitions are a motivating and major part of any person's life. It is important to note that in order to set and reach any worthwhile endeavor, individuals must first establish a pattern, a moral code, or guide of principles that allows one to remain on course and achieve their goals. One of Joe's greatest passions is understanding and protecting principles of freedom and liberty. This is not only essential to individual growth and prosperity, but also vital in building any successful community. He has found through personal experience that adhering to principles, life is no longer left to chance.

As an avid reader and student of the Founding Fathers, Joe has come to love and appreciates the freedoms, liberties, and opportunities that are available to all men and women. In addition to religious and civic responsibilities throughout his history, Joe holds strongly to the belief that every individual is important and within them, contain great achievement once their unique ability is unlocked and developed. It is this philosophy and mindset that drives he as a family to stretch even further.

He and his wife continue to educate their children, and seek to do so with those around them on these principles. He continually strives each day to improve and strengthen their family, community, and country. As an artist, author, designer, poet, songwriter, and teacher, it is his life experiences which foster an environment for creative thinking and innovation. This affords the wonderful opportunity to connect with individuals from all walks of life for the sole purpose of lifting those around him.

www.ingramcontent.com/pod-product-compliance
Lightning Source LLC
Chambersburg PA
CBHW060845280326
41934CB00007B/929